G000123380

LEAVE 'EM
SPEECHLESS

How To Conquer Your Fear
Of Public Speaking And Turn It
Into Your Most Powerful Weapon

Tom Zalaski

Nantucket Sleighride Productions

Copyright 2015

Copyright 2015 by Tom Zalaski

Published in the United States by Nantucket Sleighride Productions.

Worldwide distribution facilitated for Nantucket Sleighride Productions by Amazon.com, Amazon Kindle, Barnes and Noble and TomZalaski.com.

All rights reserved. No part of this book may be reproduced by any mechanical, photographic, or electronic process, or in the form of a photographic recording; nor may it be stored in a retrieval system, transmitted, or otherwise be copied for public or private use – other than for "fair use" as brief quotations embodied in articles and reviews – without prior written permission of the publisher.

Library of Congress Cataloging-In-Publication Data

Zalaski, Tom
    Leave 'Em Speechless : How To Conquer Your Fear Of Public Speaking And Turn It Into Your Most Powerful Weapon / Tom Zalaski. – 1st ed.
ISBN 978-0-9789223-3-7 (paperback)
ISBN 0-9789223-3-6 (Amazon Kindle)

Paperback ISBN 978-0-9789223-3-7
Amazon Kindle0-9789223-3-6

Printed in the United States of America

TABLE OF CONTENTS

Chapter 1: Mic Check 1

Chapter 2: Why Are You Here? 5

Chapter 3: They're Sellin' Stuff! 8

Chapter 4: The Step Beyond 12

Chapter 5: False Evidence Appearing Real 22

Chapter 6: The Fear Of The Unfriendly Skies 24

Chapter 7: The Room Of 1000 Demons 30

Chapter 8: The Gym, Judgment And Your Jailer 34

Chapter 9: How An NFL Star Tackled Fear 39

Chapter 10: The Tethered Elephant 43

Chapter 11: Let's Change Pain To Pleasure 45

Chapter 12: Wolves 53

Chapter 13: Tiptoe Through The Amygdala 54

Chapter 14: Change The Meaning! 58

Chapter 15: Mississippi Queen 62

Chapter 16: Believe You Are Unstoppable! 63

Chapter 17: Disaster And Diets 65

Chapter 18: Six Figures Or Eight Figures? Speaking Figures! 71

Chapter 19: A Tool For Good Or Evil 73

Chapter 20: Know Thine Audience 74

Chapter 21: "Tom, The Colonel Is Here." 76

Chapter 22: A 'Rocky' Start 78

Chapter 23: Oh My God, You Scared Me! 81

Chapter 24: Dyadic Transactional Communication 83

Chapter 25: The Finish Line – Let's Get Physical! 86

Chapter 26: The Script 89

Chapter 27: Your Best Friend 93

Chapter 28: Tips That Could Save Your Life! 96

Chapter 29: Rehearse 98

Chapter 30: Do You Know The Way To San Jose? 101

Chapter 31: Watch Your Step, Your Cell And Don't Be A Heel 103

Chapter 32: The Microphone Mystery Solved 105

Chapter 33: Soundcheck Like A Rockstar! 109

Chapter 34: Hey, I Sound Pretty Good! 110

Chapter 35: Turn Me On 111

Chapter 36: A Final Soundoff About Sound 113

Chapter 37: Let There Be Light 114

Chapter 38: "You Can't Have 'Dem Lights!" 116

Chapter 39: Take A Stand, Then Take A Bow 118

Chapter 1:

Mic Check

***A journey of a thousand miles begins
with a single step.***
- Lao Tsu

"Testing one, two, three. Is this mic on?" Hi friend! Welcome to Leave 'Em Speechless, a book designed to not only get you through that next speech but to get you to that next level where not only do you no longer fear public speaking but it's something you actually look forward to because somehow you got kinda good at it! That's where I want you and me to go with this.

I want you to know first that I have tremendous respect for you. I don't know where you are in your journey to get over your fear of public speaking. Maybe you're just a bit nervous or on edge before you have to speak before a group. Perhaps public speaking terrifies you and you're scared to death to get up in front of a group to speak! That's ok! Here's all that matters. Whatever level you're at you're doing something about it. You're trying. As with all things in life anything you try and you stick with you'll reach your goal. You will be successful.

You're different than the rest!Most people who are afraid of speaking in public have a wonderful way of dealing with their fear – they simply avoid speaking in public! Anytime there's a possibility they may have to address a group or organization or God forbid a convention, they always come up with an excuse about why they can't. They claim they're not qualified or they don't know the subject matter well enough. Did you know that some people even schedule vacations in order to avoid having to speak in public?

What you resist persists

And yes, what you've heard is true. Survey after survey has shown that most people say they would rather die than speak before a group. So, I suppose that means if they were at a funeral they'd rather be in the casket than give the eulogy! But that's where you're different. You're not coming up with excuses, you're not hiding or taking a vacation or doing whatever else to avoid doing a public speech. You've told yourself,"Enough! I'm going to face this thing. I'm going to get over this fear and if I don't get completely *cured* at least I'm going to be able to manage this."

Give yourself credit for taking a positive, proactive approach for professional and personal reasons. Think of yourself as the embodiment of the adage "an ounce of prevention is worth a pound of cure." We all know people who refuse to go to the doctor no matter how sick they are or how badly something hurts. Then, when the condition becomes unbearable to the point they are forced to see a doctor, they're told it's too late. They learned that the minor twinge in their hip that started two years ago will now require a total hip replacement. Worse, they learned the minor stomach pain they ignored six months ago is now advanced colon cancer.

This is where you are different. You felt a twinge called 'fear of public speaking.' But instead of ignoring it and letting it build until it was an all-consuming fear, you decided to deal with it while it is still in its infancy.

The bottom line is you are not sick and there is nothing wrong with you. You just want to be healthier than you already are!

Nothing gets better until you admit something is wrong

So let me thank you for putting your trust in me. I've put everything I have into this book including all the rituals and steps that I use personally. But just because I've given you everything I have doesn't mean you have to accept all of it as gospel. If something I say doesn't make sense to you, sounds ridiculous, foolish or just doesn't feel right, that's ok. Skip it and move on! To be honest with you you're only going to need and use about twenty percent of what's between these covers. Twenty percent is all you're going to need to elevate yourself to a level of public speaking that most people will never come close to reaching. If you decide to really go for it and use eighty percent or all the way to one hundred percent, then welcome to public speaking's professional ranks!

My reward will be if someday I get an email from you saying, "I was scared to death to speak in public. I got your book to prepare for a presentation and I Left 'Em Speechless!" That, my friend, is the greatest gift I could ever receive.

Let's go beat this thing. And let's have some fun while we're at it, ok?

Anything you focus on and take consistent action toward, you will get good at.

Chapter 2:

Why Are You Here?

Anything we do in life is for one of two reasons.
Inspiration or Desperation
Get Inspired!

I don't know what happened to you that brought us together. Something did. You reached a breaking point that made you say, "Enough! I'm not putting up with this anymore!"

For some people the breaking point came when they *had* to do a presentation because keeping their job depended upon it. For other people the breaking point came when they disappointed *themselves* personally and they were no longer willing to live with that kind of pain. Sure, they may have been passed over for a promotion because their public speaking skills weren't where they needed to be. But what did that really cost? Perhaps a small bump in pay, maybe a meaningless title or a bruised ego. Nothing you can't recover from.

Business be damned. How about the important things in life?

I'll bet the real breaking point for you came because of something personal. Something painful. Was it your dream to toast your sister at her wedding and tell her how you really felt about her but you couldn't find the courage to do it? Have you punished yourself for twenty years because you really wanted to say a few words at Grandma's wake service but you were too afraid? Do you still kick yourself about Bill's retirement party? You worked with Bill for years but you just didn't have it in you to wish him well publicly in front of your co-workers.

Stop beating yourself up! That's all in the past and no matter how much you fret over past regrets and relive them you can't change them. But the future – that's a different story. You *can* write the story the way you want it to be and you've already started.

Public speaking is your key to fully participating in the important things in life and not just business.

I'm not as interested in what brought you here as I am about the fact that you're here. You have an issue with public speaking and you've decided to do something about it. Once you decide to do anything all you have to do it attach emotion, persistence and action to it and you will succeed.

> ***You don't have to see the whole staircase. Just take the first step.***
> ***Martin Luther King Jr.***

How many times have you heard someone (maybe you) say, "I'll quit smoking when I get motivated." Or, " I'll workout when I get motivated." Or, "I'll start saving money when I get motivated."

Guess what? Motivation is never going to just suddenly show up. You are not going to get out of bed one day and say, "Hey, I'm motivated!" You must understand that Action comes *before* Motivation. Once you begin to take action you'll get motivated and not the other way around.

You're doing it right now. You took action by buying this book. After you've assimilated the information in this book you'll be motivated to want to speak in public. You took the small step. You took action. Here comes motivation!

Action Comes Before Motivation

Chapter 3:

They're Sellin' Stuff!

I know that in your quest for answers to overcome your fear of public speaking you no doubt searched the internet for information. So have I. It's overwhelming and frustrating, isn't it? You've gone to websites, read articles and watched YouTube videos that usually directed you to the hundreds of so-called 'speaking coaches' whose real goal is to sell you a DVD program, an internet course, a webinar or ebook all with a '3 Easy Payment' plan, right? These self-described 'coaches' either are business consultants, motivational speakers, college speech professors or former Mary Kay sales representatives. Their area of expertise is not public speaking. Their area of expertise is sellin' stuff and they're darned good at it!And now they want to sell *you* stuff! They all promise to give you the formula for the perfect speech. They tell you how to open your speech, how to close your speech, what should go into the body of the speech plus all the buzzwords to say and hot buttons to press to make your audience buy whatever it is that you're selling whether it be a product or a message.

I know you sat in front of your computer screen looking at these websites and you screamed in frustration, "No! No! No! I don't want to know how to give the perfect speech. I'm scared to death to get up on stage! I just want somebody to help me get over my fear of getting up in front of people. That's all I want!"

Before I began writing this book I wanted to make sure I was qualified to give you the information you needed. After all, I have only anchored 50,000 television newscasts, emceed hundred and hundreds of events and conducted countless media and speech seminars, so I wanted to know where I stood in the field of the so-called 'speaking coaches.' I hit the internet to see what was out there and what I found was both comical and borderline criminal.

First, I found the website offer for a "One-On-One with a board certified practitioner." Really? What's this 'board'? I sure as heck never heard of it. Who certified this guy? And he's a practitioner of *what*? There's snake oil written all over this one!

At the next website I found the services of a 'business consultant' who could help you with your speech issues. Really? He may know business but what qualifies a business consultant to help you with the fear of speaking? One woman touted her experience in telephone sales and management as her qualifications to be able to help you. Really?

The next website required an initial $75 investment followed by two months of payments of $75. It wasn't real clear what you were getting for your $225. Then there was the 'Anxiety Coach' who wanted $39.95. Then there was the website that offered to get you over your 'Performance Anxiety' for $400! I was most intrigued by the website that promised, "For $19.95 you'll learn the secrets only the pros know." Such mystery! I didn't know there were any secrets.

I particularly enjoyed the website that wanted to sell you a drug called Bravia. Bravia. As in 'Brave'? Heck, I'll sell you a bottle of Jack Daniels. Your speech won't go very well but I guarantee you won't be afraid! Seriously, don't ever rely on drugs or alcohol to deal with your public speaking issue.

The few books I found on the subject were mostly filled with busy work. Each chapter ended with Action Steps and of course there was the Workbook – all of which you don't have time for. Action Steps and Workbooks simply add pages to the book to make you think you're getting a lot for your money.

Then I checked out the videos these 'coaches' and 'consultants' posted on YouTube. What I saw ranged from amateurish to "I recorded this in my mother's basement" creepy. One video featured soothing music and clouds. Let me promise you that on the day of your speech when you get to the podium there will be no music or clouds!

I understand that you're not looking to make an investment of money and time for a year, or six months or even three months. You need the information right now because your speech is coming up in a matter of weeks. That's why I'm glad you're here. You get it all right now. This is one-stop shopping.

Sarcasm aside, there weren't very many ads or videos of people who could actually help you except to help you part with your money.

I understand your frustration. To make an analogy, it's like a master chef saying to you, "I can show you how to make the perfect pot of chili." To which you reply, "Great, but I'm scared to death to go into the kitchen! Get me into the kitchen first, then we'll talk about your chili recipe."

The information you hold in your hand right now is everything you need. It is solid, no-nonsense information and employs no psychological tricks. I'm not sellin' stuff. You don't need to put 20 lessons on your credit card. This is WD-40 and Draino. It works NOW!

For more than twenty years I have been a student and follower of several personal transformation teachers and have learned much from each. One of them, Anthony Robbins is of the opinion that people do things for one of two reasons – either inspiration or desperation. I would carry Tony's hypothesis one step further and suggest we are sometimes motivated by frustration or exasperation. That's probably what brought you here. Harness the power of these motivators. As you work to overcome your fear of public speaking, find which of these motivators causes you to take action. The surefire formula for success is to state your desire – what it is you want ("I want to be comfortable speaking before a group"), identify your purpose to give your desire power ("I will no longer deny myself the personal joy and professional success public speaking will mean") and then take massive action like you're doing right now. Get angry!

'Why' comes before 'How'.
Once you know the 'Why' you'll figure out the 'How'.

Chapter 4:

The Step Beyond

I am determined to do more for you than just give you some techniques to help you get over your fear of public speaking. Here's why. Once you are filled with courage and confidence I would be doing you a disservice if I did not show you how to use that courage and confidence properly and constructively.

For example, imagine you were afraid of water and you went to a therapist who got you over your fear of water. Do yourself a favor and don't dive off a dock into ten feet of water because although you may no longer fear water you still can't swim! You're gonna drown!

What if you were afraid to ride a horse? A therapist will easily get you over your fear of horseback riding but then don't jump up on a horse! As you lay on the ground after being thrown, you'll remember, "Oh yeah, I'm not afraid to ride a horse but I *don't know how* to ride one."

The information I'm giving you in this book is designed to get you over your fear of public speaking, but then what? You're going to need to know how to harness your newfound courage. Just because you no longer fear your audience doesn't mean you should grab a microphone and jump up on stage! No, there's a bit more to it than that! That's the *extra* I want to give you in this book. I'm going to give you *my* routine, *my* personal checklist that I use before, during and even after all of my speeches to ensure success. In fact, most professional speakers don't know even half of the tips and techniques that I'll be showing you! I'm going to give you some truly powerful and practical techniques to give your presentation that professional look.

So how does swimming and horses relate to you and public speaking? Just like getting over the fear of water or horses we will first deal with the emotional and mental components that comprise this thing we call fear. Once you face those components head-on and deal with them your fear will be greatly diminished. At that point we move on to the how-to aspects of public speaking. So put on your bathing suit and saddle up, we've got places to go and people to talk to!

I also want you to know I'm not going to waste your time with theories or hypothetical situations. As I said earlier, I'm going to give you my personal rituals and take you through every step that I take when I prepare for a speech, presentation or emcee job. So not only will you be a fearless speaker, you'll be a confident one as well because you'll know the techniques, the steps, the rituals and the game plan the professionals use so nothing is left to chance and success is guaranteed.

Let me tell you what I've got planned for you during this time we're spending together. In the first half of the book I'm going to be your cheerleader. The second half is going to be hands-on, how-to-do-it, specific, practical stuff!

Don't look for me to psychoanalyze you. I'm not a psychologist and I don't play one on TV! You're looking for something simple and effective that you can use right away.

The simple exercises that I'll give you from time to time can be done in private so you don't have to practice in front of family or friends and run the risk of embarrassing yourself. Whether it's in this course or during one of my live seminars I believe putting someone on the spot is not helpful. Calling somebody up on stage who came in with public speaking issues already only makes the situation worse. Bringing them up on stage just embarrasses them and they feel worse than they did when they came in! Instead, I'm going to use stories, lots of stories. Not because I like to hear myself tell stories but because I want to tell you about real-life situations with real-life people who faced the same challenges as you and how they overcame them. The stories are designed to assure you that you're not alone and also to convince you that you can get to where they got. I believe we learn more effectively with stories and examples. As I mentioned earlier, we're going to attack this thing on three fronts – the emotional front, the mental front and the physical front. You already know there's an emotional front to this thing otherwise you wouldn't have bought this book. It's emotional alright. You've got a certain degree of fear or anxiety that bought you here.

To deal with the emotional aspect of the fear of public speaking we're going to confront head-on that three-headed monster that's been causing you to lose sleep. This monster has a name. Your Audience. It also goes by a couple of aliases – Your Co-Workers and Your Friends. These are those horrible people who you have convinced yourself are out to criticize your every word, your every move and who will take great delight in watching you stumble, fall and fail. I hope the absurdity of this statement gives you some idea of how we're going to approach the emotional aspect of public speaking! We're simply going to change your perception of this monster and expose it for what it really is.

– that's something otherwise known as tapping, neuro associative conditioning – there are scores of methods. I've studied these and several other methods and you know what? They work! Yes. Each of these methods, when applied properly, works. They'll get you over your fear. But as I said before, once they get you over your fear, now what do you do? Don't put that bathing suit on or saddle that horse just yet! That's where this program is different. You see, my question to the practitioners of those other methods is, "Have you done it?" I would also like to ask them, "When's the last time you gave a speech?" "How often do you speak?" "After you got your client through the fear did you then move on to the next step and tell him or her what they had to do next to be successful?" Probably not because that's not what these practitioners (salesmen) do. Yes, they can talk the talk but most of them haven't walked the walk.

If at this point you're expecting me to try to impress you with a long list of credentials to make you feel better about having invested in this program I'm going to disappoint you. While I may have credentials, *my* credentials don't do *you* one bit of good. Haven't we all been faced with the credentialed 'expert' who certainly knew his stuff but failed miserably when he tried to make you understand it? I know I have. When I have to deal with the auto technician, the computer expert, the plumber or electrician I stand there cluelessly nodding my head as they overwhelm me with information and try to impress me with their foreign shoptalk. As I listen to them my mind is simply saying, "I have no idea what you just said. All I want to know is can you fix my problem? I have no idea how to fix it and the fact that you've fixed the problem for hundreds of others is of no concern to me right now. *I* have a problem and *I* need that problem fixed. Can you fix *my* problem?" This point is made so well in a book by Harry Beckwith and Christine K.

Clifford titled *You, Inc.* which is full of valuable tips on how to sell yourself in the business world. The authors talk about people who try to sell themselves, their service or their product by trying to impress prospective customers with credentials such as how long they've been in business, their degrees, their awards, some of the big name clients they've worked for and the fact that their company is about to open an office in Singapore. People don't care about your credentials. They just want a solution to their problem, that's all. Sometimes you just want to scream and say, "Open your new office in my house and fix my problem!"

That's the approach I want to take with you. While I'm aware that hundreds, maybe thousands of people are going to look to this book for help, my concern is for *you* and only *you*. You have an issue with public speaking and you and I are going to beat this thing together. The only important credential I bring to the table is my joy of speaking and my joy of helping others enjoy it as I do. I've done it. For nearly 40 years. I do it all the time. I love doing it and I love showing others how to do it! A few years ago I tried to come up with a rough estimate of how many half-hour television newscasts I had anchored in my life and I lost count after 30,000. So now, these few years later I'm probably closer to 40,000 or 50,000. Beside my television work, I'm at a podium nearly every week in front of a live audience either at an event, a seminar, a speech, a convention or an emcee job. I don't tell you this to impress you but rather to tell you I'd have to be an idiot not to know a little something about public speaking! My job, my privilege and my pleasure is to share that knowledge with you. I've made all the mistakes, believe me. So what you're getting here is not just the stuff that works but maybe more important, all the stuff that doesn't work that could lead to disaster. That's perhaps the best bonus of all!

You don't care about who else I've helped.
All you want to know is how I'm going to help you!

During our time together I will always keep in mind that you're here because you need help, you need it *now* and you don't have time to waste. You perhaps have a speech or presentation coming up in the relatively near future. I've designed this course to be one-stop shopping. You get it all and you get it now. But hey, as long as you're on a roll, don't stop! Once you've blasted through your speaking issues *go for it* and tackle those other issues in your life that you're not happy with – your finances, your health, your relationships and who you want to be spiritually and mentally. After you've gone through this program let me encourage you to take a look at other experts and their techniques that will help you break through those other fears and limitations that have been hanging over your head for years. Check out Bob Proctor, Esther Hicks, John Assaraf, Joe Vitale, Tony Robbins' *Personal Power* program and the movies *The Secret* and *What The Bleep Do We Know?* I might also recommend books like *Harmonic Wealth* by James Arthur Ray, *Excuses Begone* by Dr. Wayne W. Dyer, *The Success Principles* by Jack Canfield, *The Sedona Method* by Hale Dwoskin, Bruce Lipton's *The Biology of Belief, Think and Grow Rich* by Napolean Hill, *Infinite Possibilities* by Mike Dooley, *The Science of Getting Rich* by Wallace Wattles, *You Were Born Rich* by Bob Proctor, *Self Mastery Through Conscious Autosuggestion* by Emile Coue, *The Magic of Thinking Big* by David J. Schwartz, Ph.D. and the aforementioned *You, Inc.* by Harry Beckwith and Christine K. Clifford.

What all of these experts teach is that you can *be, do or have* anything you want by making some simple changes in the way you think. They also teach that whatever circumstances you find yourself in right now, you brought them upon yourself. You're the cause. You're the author. No one did anything to you. You did it to yourself and by that same logic, you can change anything you want to. It's all an inside job! All of these people have some great information on how to have fun with your brain and to get more out of yourself than you ever dreamed possible.

So, as I said, I'm not a psychiatrist or a psychologist and I don't play one on TV so I can't sit here and tell you that I'm going to absolutely cure you of your fear of speaking in public. But what I do feel comfortable telling you is that we're going to get you to that next level, ok? So, if you're deathly afraid of public speaking and can't even look at a podium (and boy, have I got my own story about airplanes you'll read about later) we're at least going to get you up to the podium and get you through your speech or presentation. You still may not love it but you're going get through it. If you're at the stage where speaking in public is like going to the dentist – you know, ya gotta do it so you do it and get it over with – we want to move you up on the scale to where you're not only comfortable with it but you're pretty good at it and in the end you're proud of yourself. Or perhaps you're a seasoned public speaker and your job is such that you're in front of people all the time. Let's get you to that next level – from being just good to the point where you not only look forward to doing it but people look forward to hearing you.

In the title of Chapter 2 I asked, Why Are You Here? The real answer is that you are the product of your past patterns of thinking. Your past thoughts have created who and what you are today. So what logically follows is that the thoughts you are thinking right now are creating your future. Your past thoughts and associations about public speaking are what bought you to your current feelings about getting up before a crowd. From this point forward let's change those thoughts and associations. In doing so you will change your public speaking future *beginning this moment*!

As I said earlier, I also hope you will use the information in this book to apply to other areas of your life. The same techniques that get you over the fear of public speaking can also be applied to other areas of your life where you might be hesitating such as starting a new business, beginning a new hobby or even writing a book!

It's time to put out the fear fire.
Stick your head into the fire hose and drink!

Chapter 5:

False Evidence Appearing Real

Why Do Those Horrible People Want Me To Fail?

Alright, it's time to get down to business. Let's tackle this thing and get it under control so that instead of dreading it, speaking becomes an effective tool in your professional life *and* your personal life. I said we are going to attack this thing on three fronts – the emotional, mental and physical. So let's start with the emotional. And this is emotional stuff. Hey, I know what you've missed out on. As we talked about earlier, you wanted to get up and speak at your sister's wedding reception, you wanted to get up and say a few kind words at your parent's anniversary party or your friend's retirement party but you were afraid to do it and now you're regretting not doing it because you wish you had.

One of the best ways I've learned to get you comfortable in facing any fear, whatever it may be, is to let you know you're not alone. So I want to do that by relating to you a few stories about yours truly and people I either know or have worked with and how they faced and conquered fear.

When you focus on a fear it disappears

I may not know *your* fear but I do know fear. Fear is fear is fear and it doesn't matter what you're afraid of because it all feels the same. But you know what fear really is – fear – F.E.A.R. False Evidence Appearing Real. Let me say that again – False Evidence **Appearing** Real. Let me give you an example and I'll use myself. I don't know your fear but as I said, I do know fear.

Chapter 6:

The Fear Of The Unfriendly Skies

This story is personal and painful but ultimately turned into a pleasurable victory which is how I want your fear of speaking story to ultimately end!

For 30 years I deprived myself of the joy, freedom, speed and efficiency of air travel. I was *deathly* afraid to fly. Remember I said most people would rather die than speak in public? Well, when it came to flying, I'd rather die than fly! In my twisted thinking this made sense because if I got on that airplane I was going to die. Sadly for me that belief meant that for years, whenever my family and I would take a vacation a long way from home we'd have to go either by car or train – 24 hours on the road instead of a wonderful two-hour plane flight to our destination. It was the same thing in business life. I work in television news. Certain stories require us to go to far-off places and we need to get there now! Like on an airplane. It meant that I had to decline covering many wonderful, exciting and even history-making events because my television station needed someone there now! It pains me to think about what those 30 years of irrational fear deprived me of both professionally and personally.

Those 30 years of fear and deprivation came to an abrupt end on one frightening, gut-wrenching and life-changing day. I got trapped and there was no way out except to face my fear of flying head-on and deal with it just like you're doing right now with your fear of public speaking. Here's what happened. I'm sure you've seen on your local television stations where the weather guy or one of the other station personalities does a commercial for a vacation getaway – you know, inviting viewers to join him and his wife on a fabulous week in Maui or the Rockies, Italy, France and even New Zealand. Not only do these vacations come at no expense to the personality and his spouse or friend but the excursion doesn't even come off your vacation time because the television station considers it work! Technically, you're working as you entertain and play host to forty people who have paid big money to come on the trip. Although my television colleagues regularly hosted these trips and got extra vacation time in the process I never asked to host a trip for obvious reasons – I didn't want to fly. Boy, talk about missing the boat on about 30 years of free vacations!

The beginning of the end came for me when one of my newsroom colleagues and his wife were scheduled to host such a trip – this one to Austria and Germany! They were scheduled to visit Salzburg including Mirabell Gardens where part of the movie *Sound of Music* was filmed, Kitzbuhel, Innsbruck and Munich where they'd get to go to the real Octoberfest! However, two months before the trip, my colleague left our station for another job. The tour company – Holiday Vacations – needed what they call a 'celebrity' host to replace him. My boss called me into his office. I sat down and from across the desk he pushed this beautiful color travel brochure toward me that said *Austria and Germany*! He said, "I wondered if you'd like to take Chris's place on this trip?"

I freaked! I heard what he asked, I saw the brochure, I went into panic mode and it took me less than a second to give him my answer – "No, Lee. I can't. I can't fly!" He couldn't believe what he was hearing! But before accepting my emphatic refusal he said, "Well, why don't you call Wendy and see what she says." Wendy is love-of-my-life and better-half Wendy. I walked to my desk and picked up the phone. I knew right then and there it was over – this fear of flying thing had to end and end now. Could I really deprive Wendy, not to mention myself, of an all-expense-paid, once-in-a-lifetime trip to Austria and Germany? Oh sure, in the back of my mind I was hoping when I told Wendy about the trip she'd say, "Oh, I'd never force you to do that. You can't fly." Not a chance. Wendy is understanding but not *that* understanding. I called her, told her that the station wanted me to host this trip and the first words out of her mouth were "You have to go!" As if I didn't know that was going to be her response.

Reality hit. I had to beat this fear or at least manage it. Fortunately, a young lady who worked at our television station learned of my dilemma and said to me, "My mom is a therapist. She works with fear of flying all the time. Go see her." So I did – for about 10 weekly sessions. Without doing a virtual lobotomy on me she gave me some good advice such as when I thought about flying to think about the one place on earth where I am happiest and associate the fact that flying could take me to that happy place quickly. The objective was for me to change what I associated flying to. Rather than associate flying to ultimate fear I would link flying to being the means by which I could quickly get to my happiest place on earth. The therapist also gave me a couple of practical tips which sounded like they'd really work. First, she suggested I bring an Ipod loaded with either my favorite music or something motivational like a Tony Robbins session. She suggested that I begin listening before takeoff while the plane was still on the runway. Then, when the plane actually did take off I would just continue listening, my audio environment wouldn't change and I wouldn't really notice too much that I was leaving earth. She also said to use Wendy as a calming effect during the flight. Hold hands. Talk to her. It was another way to get my mind off the fact that I was airborne. OK, so I was all set for the big day. IPod loaded and Wendy was with me. Fear of flying -- you have met your match.

But two little problems came up. First, we boarded this huge, trans-Atlantic jumbo jet only to discover Wendy and I didn't have seats together! I was in one section, she was in another and no matter how hard we tried, the people sitting next to her and those sitting next to me didn't want to change seats with us. Oh, boy. Well, OK, plan B. At least I had my IPod. So I fired it up, concentrating on the motivational talk, concentrating hard so I wouldn't notice that I was taking off and leaving this planet. But just before takeoff the flight attendant's voice came over the airplane's intercom system asking everyone to please turn off all electronic devices until we were at cruising altitude! So there I was, no Wendy, no IPod, no drugs, not even any alcohol service until 30,000 feet and I had a 5000 mile, nine-and-a-half hour flight ahead of me.

There is nothing rational about fear.
We're all a little bit crazy, admit it!
Snakes, heights, flying, spiders and speaking.
You're normal!

So how does my fear-of-flying story relate to you? Fear is relative. You got this book because the way you feel about public speaking is the same way I felt about airplanes! You're probably saying, "Tom, the flight to my convention is a piece of cake! It's the speech I gotta give when I get there that's scarin' me to death!"

You know what's particularly sad about a fearful flyer? It's not just the actual flight you're afraid of. Oh no. Your fear starts the minute you realize that you're going to have to fly somewhere. The date of the trip could be three months away but it doesn't matter because your fear starts the minute you find out you're going. Even worse, let's say this flight is taking you, your spouse and four of your best friends on that trip to Hawaii you've all been talking about for years. First, you have to endure the terror of the flight to Honolulu on the premise of enjoying a week in heaven. But for the fearful flyer, when you get there it's not a week in heaven. It's a week in hell because you know that no matter what, when this week comes to an end, you have to get back on that plane. It consumes you and ruins your entire vacation.

This is exactly what happens to people who are afraid of speaking in public. Your company wants to send you and your spouse to a convention in, let's say, San Francisco. You happen to live in Hartford, Connecticut so San Francisco would be a wonderful new experience. You also know that at the typical convention you are required to attend one or two seminars each day and the rest of the time is yours to relax and sightsee. The best part is it's all on the company's dime! The not nice thing is that at one of these seminars, you're the presenter! So just like the fearful flyer, your fear or discomfort begins the day you are told you're going to the convention to give a presentation for your company. In the weeks or months leading up to the big trip your spouse can't contain his or her excitement. San Francisco, Fisherman's Wharf, the Golden Gate Bridge, Alcatraz, seafood and those iconic trolley cars. Oh, the fun! But you see it differently. Amidst all the buildup and excitement, you're saying, "Just shoot me now and put me out of my misery." All you can think about is the presentation you have to do and that thought is already ruining what should be a fabulous trip. The best you can hope for is that your presentation is on the first day of the convention so you can get it over with and enjoy the rest of the week.

If this is you, the first thing I want you to know is, "It's OK!" What makes the problem worse is we build it up in our heads and we think we're the only one who has this fear, nobody else feels this way and there's no solution. The fact is, if you look around you, nine out of ten people you work with or deal with each day have the same fear – probably worse! As I said before, here's the big difference between you and them. You've admitted it. And remember, *nothing ever gets better until you admit something is wrong.* Not only are you admitting it but you're facing it head on and you're doing something about it.

Action Cures Fear! Take action on anything you fear and watch the fear disappear.

Chapter 7:

The Room Of 1000 Demons

I came across a wonderful story about breaking through fear. It has been told many different ways but here is the version I like best and share with you. The story is called *The Room of 1000 Demons*.

Once upon a time, in an ancient world not so far from here, there was a tradition. Every one hundred and one years, any who wanted could undertake the challenge. If you survived the challenge you would gain enlightenment. Since the ritual was offered every one hundred and one years, if you didn't embrace the challenge you would have to wait for one hundred and one more years to take it again. It was a challenge with some bite to it.

All the applicants were gathered in the great hall, wearing their best robes, standing as still as their nervousness would permit. Compassionately, the priests explained the ritual to these assembled applicants who were already fully apprised of the ritual in all its detail. But this final time they were facing the ritual itself, facing their future and facing the doors at the end of the great hall. The priest intoned, "You will line up and one by one you will pass through the door at the end of this hall and enter the room beyond. The room beyond is the Room of 1000 Demons." Almost as one, the applicants turned and looked at the huge wooden doors at the east end of the hall. You could hear a collective inhale followed by a sigh as they turned. Continuing, the priest spoke, "The Room of 1000 Demons is not so big but there are no handles on the inside of those doors. Once you pass through the doors they will close behind you. The only way out is to cross the room and discover the door on the other side. It is unlocked. Simply walk out." He had the applicants' full focus now.

He went on, "You know by now that the Room of 1000 Demons is named that way for good reason. The room is filled with 1000 demons. These demons are powerfully skilled in their ability to take on the form of your worst fears. They are merciless. If you fear spiders you will have them crawling on your face. If it is heights that make your knees jelly you will be looking down into the abyss from the most rickety of walkways. If it is failure you fear well, you can imagine. Whatever your worst fears are, they will meet you on the other side of that door."

Some of the applicants seemed to pale. Others had just slunk out of the great hall. One person had to be carried out while the others' eyes were riveted on the doorway or else turned inwards towards their fears. Again, the priest spoke. This time more kindly. "These demons are so skilled and compelling it will be nearly impossible to remember they are not real. They are cunningly *your* demons. Remember, we can't come to your aid. You must complete the challenge on your own. Some applicants never leave the room. They succumb to their paralyzing fears and stay until the end of their days. You must choose to take the risk or not. Either choice is fine. If you choose to decline the challenge this time you can return in one hundred and one years and apply again. There is good news. We have two hints for you. First, starting from the initial moment inside the door, the very moment the door closes behind you, remember that what the demons show you is not real. But note this well – most people find it very difficult to remember that these are illusions. They appear perfectly real and they are, of course, tailored to fit you perfectly. So here's the second hint. It is more helpful. Once you are in the room and the door closes behind you, no matter what appears before you, no matter what you feel or what you think, keep your feet moving. If you keep your feet moving no matter what you will eventually get to the other side, discover the door and come out of the room enlightened." The priest finished and gestured toward the doors. In deep silence, one by one, each applicant stood before the huge doors, took a calming breath and entered the Room of 1000 Demons.

End of story.

Did you find it interesting that a line you read a minute ago said, "They appear perfectly real, and they are, of course, tailored to fit you perfectly." Appear perfectly real. Kind of like what we talked about before – Fear. F-E-A-R. False Evidence Appearing Real.

You have been through these doors before. You've crossed the room and came out the other side. My goodness, you left home for college. That was a little scary but you did it. Same with that first job – you went in with no experience and only the desire to make it and you did. How about getting married? Or having kids? You had no idea what was up that road but you took the chance and I know you're glad you did. Against all odds you did all of it. You've already been through the hard part!

So now you're facing your next fear. You knew that by investing in this book you were going to have to go through the door where your fear of public speaking would be waiting for you. Just remember, it's False Evidence Appearing Real. Keep your feet moving and you're going to walk out of the door on the other side of the room with a sense of pride, accomplishment and excitement. You're facing your fear and you're doing something about it. Most others avoid it at all costs and never face it. They're the ones who have succumbed to their paralyzing fears and they'll be stuck in the Room of 1000 Demons until the end of their days.

So, let me just reinforce it again – I don't know your fear but I do know fear and best of all I do know you're going to break through it.

The only thing preventing you from reaching your goal is the story you tell yourself as to why you can't have it.

Chapter 8:

The Gym, Judgment And Your Jailer

We've established that emotion is a big part of the fear of public speaking equation. But I hope you feel better about yourself now knowing that you're not alone. We all have fears and you're OK. Kind of like that book 'I'm OK, You're OK!' We're all OK! So with that in mind let's stop beating ourselves up. It's important for you to feel good about yourself and to be comfortable with where you are and how you're feeling because that's going to be important as we tackle the second part of dealing with the fear of public speaking – the Mental Aspect. We're going to spend a lot of time on this because in everything we do in life we're essentially playing a mental game with ourselves – "Can I or can't I, will I or won't I?" We have to change the association of not only what giving a speech means to us but we also have to change our perception of the audience, the people listening to us.

In your mind you have probably linked up some pretty strong negative associations to what public speaking means to you and how your audience will see you. Your mind is telling you, "Public speaking is scary and my audience is out to get me and they only showed up to watch me embarrass myself."Well, we're going to change those associations. First, a look at how we made those associations in the first place.

I believe the number one reason people are afraid of public speaking is because they're afraid of being judged by their peers. "What are they gonna say about me?" For some reason we think that when we get up to give a speech or presentation everyone in the audience is critiquing our every word and move. We think everyone is watching us like a hawk, just waiting for us to make that one mistake so they can criticize us – or laugh at us – or shake their heads and say, "Oh God, that's terrible."

It's kind of like those health club commercials on radio or TV where they try to get you to join for ten dollars a month. They advertise themselves as the Judgment Free Zone. Big Voice Announcer comes on and says, "Are you tired of the muscle heads at the gym – you know, the ones who give you that look like – what's a wimp like you doing here? – Tired of getting stared at by Suzy Spandex who has no body fat and doesn't sweat?" You've heard those commercials, right? Some of these places call themselves the 'gym without the attitude.' They're playing on your fear of being judged. The club then invites you to join because they're judgment free – nobody will stare at you or make fun of you. Isn't it interesting how we feel that everyone is waiting to jump on us and criticize us? I can't count the number of people I've talked to over the years who want to work out, know they should work out, but they don't dare set foot in the gym because they're too fat or not in shape and are afraid they will be judged or criticized.

Trust me, I was there. In 1996 at the ripe old age of 43 I decided I'd better start working out on a regular basis but I hesitated to join the YMCA. Why? Because I was going to be judged by the muscle heads and Suzy Spandex or at least that's what I had convinced myself of. And then one day I got angry. Not at the muscle heads and not at Suzy but at myself. I said,"Tom, just because you think somebody's going to judge you, you're not going to join the Y. You're going to stay out of shape. You're going to risk heart disease. You'll cut your life short and deny yourself the fun and satisfaction of physical fitness. You'll probably wind up leaving your family and loved ones 20 years too soon all because you're worried about what somebody might think? Boy, that's giving people an awful lot of power over you. And what are *their* qualifications to be able to judge *you*? Well, (I reasoned) they can lift heavy things and run forever, non-stop on a treadmill." Great qualifications to be able to judge somebody, huh?

So I joined and now all these years later I'm in great shape. Well, pretty good shape. I love to work out and although I'm not cut or chiseled by any means people ask me for workout advice like how did I get toned and how did I build muscle. What you might find most interesting is that those muscle heads are now my best friends and we look forward to seeing each other everyday. In our circle of workout friends if you miss a day, watch out because the next time you show up you get accused of everything from a night of drinking to an affair! Now that I *am* one of those 'judgmental muscle heads' I'll let you in on a little secret. We don't judge anyone, criticize anyone or even talk about anyone. Why? Because *we don't care*! Anyone who works out seriously is simply only into themselves and *their* workout routine and *their* pain and *their* progress. Nothing and no one else matters. Yet, so many people are afraid to try something – exercise – or a speech - because they think they'll be judged. In the end it turns out to be absolutely not the case.

***You might think you're the center of attention.
Guess what? The serious workout muscle heads
don't care what you're doing at all!***

One last word in case you really are thinking about starting a workout program but were afraid to for fear of being judged. The 'Judgment Free Zone' might make for a catchy advertising slogan but that's about all. In my 20 years of working out in several facilities including my local gym, on the road and even during international travel, I have never, ever heard or seen anyone criticize anybody, ever! Just go do it!

So what does this have to do with you and public speaking? The audience you're so afraid of speaking to are the same as the non-existent gym muscle heads – they're imaginary critics and they only exist in your head and nowhere else. Unless the people in your audience are professional speakers they can't criticize you because frankly, they wouldn't know how to give a speech. And if the truth be told, they're just glad that it's *you* up at that podium and not *them*.

We humans are strange creatures. We can be with the same group of people but depending upon the situation we can see those people as either friendly or frightening! In one situation we are completely comfortable with them and enjoy being center stage, while in the other we're scared to death. Here's what I mean. When you're standing around the water cooler at work or taking a coffee break you have no problem confiding in your co-workers about your brother's alcoholism, a problem in the bedroom, how you're contemplating divorce, that you're having an affair or that Johnny is failing in school. Truly personal stuff. Heck, at the office Christmas party you grab that karaoke microphone and belt out tunes like you're Bono or Cher or Steven Tyler! And yet, when you have to give a speech before these very same people on a topic you're an expert on, you freeze.

It's that fear thing raising its ugly head again. Fear prevents us from realizing our true potential in all things. Fear can be positive. It can serve you. It protects you from harm. But fear can also be your jailer and paralyze you when it's irrational. Fear. You give it life. You create it. And you can kill it.

Fear can serve you. It can protect you. But fear can also be your jailer.

Chapter 9:

How An NFL Star Tackled Fear

Here is another example of same crowd, different situations and very different emotional reactions. A friend of mine named Brian played linebacker for the Green Bay

Packers. Each Sunday of the NFL season he would display his talents not just to a stadium filled with 60,000, 70,000 and even 80,000 spectators but also to a television audience that sometimes numbered in the millions if the game was on Monday Night, Thursday Night or any prime time slot of football. When Brian retired from the NFL the television station I was working for at the time hired him as a sports reporter – not as the nightly sports anchor – but as a reporter who would contribute stories about pro football as well as outdoor sports like hunting and fishing. Having Brian as a member of our sports team was quite a coup for our station. He had name recognition, he was well known, well liked and obviously there wasn't much he didn't know about football. I once asked him what it was like on game day when the team comes out of the tunnel at Lambeau Field and all of a sudden there are 60-000 people cheering at the mere sight of you, your uniform and your jersey number. His answer may have sounded boastful but I completely understood what he was saying. He said, "Tommy, *you are God.*" I'm sure that's how he felt. He said players fed off the energy of the crowd and in that moment of stepping onto the field to wild cheering Brian felt like there was nothing he couldn't do.

Soon after Brian joined our television station he did a report about Packers training camp and we thought this would be a good time to put him on the news desk with us for the first time. Brian sat next to our sportscaster who told our viewers, "As you know, a former Packer is the newest member of our sports team and here's Brian now with his first report from Packers training camp, Brian?"Brian began to read his script into the camera and as he did we could hear the rattling of papers – it was his script in his shaking hands. The shaking got worse. The rattling grew louder. Then came the sweat beading up on his forehead and dripping down the sides of his face. I thought I was about to witness a 6-foot-4-inch 275-pound heart attack right there on live TV. After what I'm sure felt to Brian like two hours, his two-minute report mercifully ended. With Brian's report finished our sportscaster thanked him and we went to a commercial break. Brian collapsed backward in his chair and with a huge exhaled sigh of relief he said, "I'm done. I can't do this. I don't know how you guys can do this every night. This isn't for me." We assured him he did fine and it was his baptism by fire. He said, "I played in front of 104,000 people at the University of Michigan stadium and that was nothin' compared to this!"

Isn't that interesting? Playing before 104,000 people was nothing. Playing before a national television audience of millions – piece of cake. And yet, presenting a report on a topic he knew best and doing it in a studio where there were only the four members of our television news team along with two camera people and no one else, he almost died of fright!

Postscript. Brian went on to have a wonderfully successful career with us. He did regular reports and even hosted live football shows. I'm sure he now laughs when he thinks back to that first night's baptism by fire when he was going to quit the television business on the spot!

I've often wondered why we feel that way? Why are we afraid of each other? What happened to us during our childhood or as we grew up? Where did this insecurity come from – this lack of confidence – this feeling that we're not good enough. Isn't it interesting how much we think *others* can do and how little *we* can do?

First, let me tell you it's not your fault. You don't have a character flaw and you're not lacking some key personality ingredient or trait. You weren't born afraid of public speaking. Did you know that babies are born with only two fears – the fear of falling and the fear of loud noises. The rest is learned. There's no fear-of-public-speaking gene. No, that thought was put in your head early on, probably by some very well-meaning people like your parents, relatives or friends who were just trying to protect you from getting hurt. *They* were afraid of public speaking and every time they talked about it, it was in a negative way like, "I would never get up in front of a group." Or, "I'm not doing the wedding toast." Or, "Yeah, I'm going to Bob's retirement party but there's no way I'm getting up to say anything."You took all of this in subconsciously and you began to associate pain to public speaking, right? What more proof did you need? If the people you loved and respected were afraid to do it then it must be something you want no part of. You took their negative attitude toward public speaking as a warning – don't do it, it'll be painful! And when you hear that message enough times it gets lodged in your subconscious as a belief and an irrefutable fact. Do you know what a belief really is? It's just a thought you keep thinking over and over again. Tell yourself something enough times and you'll start to believe it. Your conscious mind may tell you logically that there is nothing to fear about public speaking. However, your subconscious mind is thousands of times more powerful than your conscious mind and no matter what your conscious mind tells you it's your subconscious mind that's calling the shots. If your subconscious mind says public speaking equals pain, you'll believe it and avoid public speaking.

Chapter 10:

The Tethered Elephant

The conditioning and programming that brought you to your current view of public speaking is much like the story of the tethered elephant. Soon after a circus elephant is born one of its legs is tethered by a short rope tied to a post to keep the animal from running away.

Yet, when the elephant grows to be two tons it is still tethered by that same small rope. Even though the elephant could easily snap the rope and run to freedom the large animal doesn't even make an attempt at freeing itself. Why? Because the elephant was conditioned from birth that as long as the rope was on its leg there was no escape. He believed it even though it was no longer true!

In his book *The Biology of Belief* Bruce Lipton, Ph. D. gives an eye-opening explanation of how we are all controlled by behavior patterns and programs downloaded into our subconscious by *other* people.

Lipton says that from the time you were born until about age seven you were susceptible to other people's programs that got downloaded into your subconscious and you didn't have the mental capacity to question what was being downloaded. Your subconscious accepted it all as fact; mom's fear of heights, dad's fear of dogs, your sister's issue with water and Uncle Bill's fear of flying.

You surmised that all of these fears must be valid and true because they were instilled in you by the people who loved you most and wanted to protect you from these horrors.

This leads to a couple of problems later in life. First, as we said earlier the subconscious mind is thousands of times more powerful than the conscious mind. So even if your conscious mind says, "I'd like to speak in public" or "I want to fly in a jet airliner to a vacation destination" your subconscious mind overrides those desires and those old downloaded fears kick in. Your willpower is no match for the power of the subconscious.

The second problem is that only about five percent of our lives are controlled by our conscious mind. The other ninety-five percent is controlled by our subconscious mind. Know what that means? You're living someone else's life ninety-five percent of the time!

There are several techniques you can use to reprogram your subconscious. These techniques are discussed in detail in several of the books I mentioned earlier. For now just take heart in knowing your fears are not your fault. You are not flawed. Also take heart in knowing you can change it.

How long have you been tethered? Did someone in your childhood tether you with their "public speaking is scary" rope and you are still believing what they told you?

Take a good hard look at who put the idea in your head. It may have been Mom, Dad, Grandpa or Uncle Bill. Where did that thinking get them? It's a safe bet that their lives are now tethered by Social Security and a monthly pension check. You can love those people but you don't want to end up like they have.

Chapter 11:

Let's Change Pain To Pleasure

We've established that just about anything we do is to either avoid pain or gain pleasure. Let's apply that truism to your issue with speaking in public. I'd be willing to bet you bought this book to avoid pain. You probably had a conversation with yourself that went something like this:

"I have to do this presentation and I'm scared to death. But since I have no choice I gotta find a way to get over this fear and somehow get through the presentation. If I don't get over the fear I'll blow the presentation, then I'll look stupid, the boss will be mad, I could get fired, I'll lose the house" and on and on, right?

Too often we act from a place of only thinking of the pain and not the pleasure. But what if you were to tell yourself a different story and focus on the pleasure instead. Here are some simple examples:

Let's start with the story we tell ourselves about why we can't work out. The mere thought of working out is cause for pain!"I'd have to get up an hour earlier. I don't have the time.I'll have to join a gym. I'll have to buy workout clothes. I'll have to learn to operate the exercise machines. I'll be sore. I'll miss my soap operas." That's a lot of pain! No wonder you're not working out.

But what if you told yourself a different story that gave new meaning to working out. " I'll finally get in shape. I'll breathe better. I'll learn new things. I can find a workout partner to enjoy this with. I'll feel better. I'll have more energy. I'll prolong my life. I won't have to worry about heart disease or diabetes."

Don't want to tackle something as overwhelming as working out right now? How about something as simple as cleaning out that spare bedroom? You know – the place where you've been stacking bags of clothes, old kitchenware, boxes of family photos, curtains and that old treadmill you promised yourself you would use everyday. Each time you open the door to this room to throw something else in there you feel a little more frustrated, more overwhelmed and more disappointed with yourself because you've been meaning to tackle this project for a year, two years and admit it – five years! Oh, the pain!

I was there, believe me! The reason I put off cleaning out my basement storage room was because it was so full I couldn't get in there! Then one day I said, "Enough!" I gave the task new meaning. "If I clean out this basement I'll have more room, I'll be organized, I'll find things I've been missing for years and the stuff I donate is going to make for one heck of a nice tax write off." The task I had attached so much pain to for years was finished in about three hours simply by replacing painful thoughts with pleasurable ones. My pain had turned to pleasure. The room was organized, immaculate and I bagged up all my useless clothes and junk and hauled it all to Goodwill and the Salvation Army. I had more room than I knew what to do with!

We gave new meaning to working out. We gave new meaning to cleaning out the basement. So now, let's give new meaning to speaking in public. I would guess that you bought this book for painful and negative reasons. You were afraid of public speaking, you reached the end of your rope and you *had* to do something to avoid any more pain.

Let's change that right now. First, forget the subtitle of this book, "How To Conquer Your Fear Of Public Speaking And Turn It Into Your Most Powerful Weapon."

Instead, use this title: "Leave 'Em Speechless – How To Get Money, Respect, Position, Power, Authority and Control." Feels different, doesn't it? Now you're on the offensive. Instead of protecting yourself from something painful you are now aggressively going after something. Now you're saying, "I want it, I demand it, give me that stuff." Now you're ready to harness these simple, powerful tools that will send you off in a whole new direction.

I do not mean to give the impression that this power, control and authority are to be used as a club to wield over your co-workers. No, this new, aggressive approach of yours is not to put them *down* but rather to raise yourself *up*.

Every company needs a front person, the one who gets out front and pushes the company's product, line, message or cause. You can have the best product, best message, best line or best cause in the world but if you can't take that story to the public it's worthless.

Be that person and the rewards will follow – personally, professionally and financially. Management will look to you for help in moving the company forward and taking the company's story to the public. Co-workers as well as management will look to you for help. You will become the authority people look to. Why? Because you gave that impression. Remember, perception is reality. People will believe you are who you tell them you are and who you show yourself to be.

You were born to control affairs.
Let someone else be scared.

You now may be thinking, "Wait a minute Tom. This is a little too psychoanalytical. Nobody put that fear in my head – I just know from experience and talking to other people that public speaking is scary and I want nothing to do with it!" But here's what's interesting and here's how I know that your fears were planted in your brain by someone else. It works the other way, too! What are you good at? What do you love to do? What are your hobbies? What do you do for recreation? Did you know that those things were also planted in your brain – by someone else – someone who loved you, cared about you and wanted to share with you the things they enjoyed?

Let's take your Dad for instance. You overheard him talking about never wanting to get up in front of a crowd. He wouldn't propose that wedding toast and there was no way he was going to speak at Bob's retirement party. To Dad, this was frightening stuff, right?

But Dad loved hunting. And you probably do too. It's because of the way Dad talked about hunting, how he approached it, lived it and loved it. You see, he could have taken a negative approach to hunting and told you that guns were dangerous, killing animals was immoral, there were hidden dangers in the woods and hunting camp was just a place where guys got drunk and told tall tales. But no, Dad imparted to you the joy of the woods, the thrill of seeing wild animals in their natural habitat, the camaraderie of the hunting camp and the bonding not just with fellow hunters but with nature as well.

That put a different spin on hunting, didn't it? That's why you enjoy it. In fact, where I live we have an annual nine-day gun deer season each November and in the weeks and days leading up to it hunters come down with a condition affectionately called Buck Fever! They just can't wait for the season to begin and in the weeks leading up to the big day they eat, breathe and sleep the upcoming hunt.

Maybe you're not a hunter, but I'll bet there are one or more activities you take part inthat you enjoy because at some point someone with influence in your life talked about the activity, enjoyed it, wanted to share the fun with you and that's how your positive view of the activity got planted in your subconscious.

So, there are some powerful emotions involved when we're dealing with public speaking. The most powerful one being fear. Fear of being judged. Fear of being criticized. Fear of not being good enough. Fear of what others will say or think.

And I'll bet something else is true about you. Almost anything you've ever tried in your life, I mean really gave it your best effort and persisted, you probably got pretty good at. This could be recreationally or professionally. Let's say you love boating – you own a boat – you've got it docked at a marina and you can't wait for summer to come so you can enjoy that boat every weekend. There's probably not much you don't know about your boat such as how to maintain it and operate it. You know all the rules of the waterways and in your circle of boating friends you're probably viewed as master of the high seas. Now think back. Wasn't there a time you didn't know the bow from the stern? Fore from aft? Maybe you even put the lifejacket on backwards! But you learned. You kept at it. You persisted. You gave it your all and look where you are today. This is true about so many things in your life – things you were at first hesitant to try but you gave it a sincere shot and now you're pretty good if not great at it. Skiing, golfing, kayaking. How about your job? Wasn't there a time when you said, "Oh boy, I don't know if I can do this." And look where you are now – at the top of your profession and can probably do your job blindfolded!

There's a simple reason you're good at the things you're good at and a reason you're not so good at other things. It's the principle of Pain and Pleasure. Anything we do in life we do for one of two reasons – to either avoid Pain or to gain Pleasure. The things you're good at you probably associate pleasure to. The reason you avoid certain situations is because you associate pain to them. You've linked up in your mind, "If I do *this* thing I'll get pleasure, but if I do *that* thing, it'll be painful."

"Every time I denied myself the experience of my own greatness it's because I moved away from rather than into my place of discomfort. Not once in a while. Not now and then. Every single time!"

Neale Donald Walsch
Author, 'Conversations With God' series

This is simply your next conquest and then you will move on to other things.

You are here to confront your fear of speaking in public. For you, public speaking carries with it a certain amount of anxiety and perhaps even panic. Yet for me, public speaking has just the opposite meaning. For me, a television studio with three cameras pointed at me and 300,000 people watching at home is my safe haven. It is my cocoon. No one can hurt me. I am protected. It is, as they say, 'my happy place.'

One person's pain can be another person's pleasure. As April 15th approaches do you look forward to the prospect of doing your taxes? I know I don't! The number 1040 is probably my least favorite number! And yet you probably know people who do their own taxes and actually enjoy it. They think it's a breeze and they get extra pleasure because they're saving money by not having to pay a tax service or an accountant. My accountant loves filing tax returns because it's what he does for a living and enjoys it! What I associate pain to he gets great pleasure out of and a nice income as well!

So, how do we apply this principle of pain and pleasure to public speaking? Simple. If you change the association you change the meaning. In other words, change what you associate public speaking to and you'll change what it means to you. I'll give you an example most people can identify with – exercise. Most people don't exercise because they associate pain to it, right? Exercise. I've used this example before and you're probably tired of it but it is so true that I want to make sure you understand my point.What does exercise – working out mean to you? Well, for most people, exercise – working out – means pain. And we rationalize, right? You've said it to yourself, "Yeah, I'm 30 pounds overweight, but ya know, I work hard and when I get home I'm beat. I have a cocktail, maybe two, eat supper, watch some TV and then it's time for bed because I gotta get up and do it all over again tomorrow."

The only thing missing in this schedule is *exercise*. Time for yourself. Time for your body. Your temple. Your health.

What if you simply changed the story you tell yourself about exercise so that instead of thinking of it in terms of pain you associate pleasure to it. What could you say to yourself? What new associations could you make? Well, for starters how about, "This isn't as hard as I'm making it out to be. All I have to do is join a club or the YMCA – maybe join with somebody – a partner, we'll have one of the trainers start us off slowly and in a matter of weeks the weight will start coming off, the excess fat will turn into toned muscle, I'll breathe better, my heart will be stronger and maybe best of all I'll feel better about myself because I took that one small step, got myself to take action and turned something I used to think was painful into something I look forward to everyday."

And don't forget, there's also something to be said for prolonging your life!

Will this work if you tell yourself this new story just one time. No! You've spent years building up your aversion to exercise so it's going to take a little while to uninstall that negative thinking. But the more you tell yourself the new story the quicker you'll forget the old way of thinking and start to create a new association to exercise. Bottom line, you'll not only turn something that was painful into pleasure but you'll get to the point where *not* working out would be painful because you'd be denying yourself all those health benefits we talked about.

Chapter 12:

Wolves

It's your choice. You can associate either pain or pleasure to public speaking. Both associations will deliver results, just very different results. Case in point, the 'Wolves' story:

One evening an old Cherokee told his grandson about a battle that goes on inside people.

He said, "My son, the battle is between two wolves inside us all. One is Evil – It is anger, jealousy, greed and arrogance. The other is Good – It is peace, love, hope, humility, compassion and faith."

The grandson thought about this for a while and then asked his grandfather, "Which wolf wins?"

To which the old Cherokee replied, "The one I feed."

Public speaking can either continue to bring you pain or it can deliver great pleasure. Which will you feed?

Chapter 13:

Tiptoe Through The Amygdala

Why is it that when we try to achieve a goal that is really important to us we go into a state of overwhelm? Instead of moving us toward the goal our brain seems to just shut down. We're paralyzed.

We all experienced this when we studied really hard for that super-important exam and then on the day of the test our mind went blank and we couldn't remember a thing.

Learning to get over the fear of public speaking is a bit overwhelming, isn't it? You feel like there is too much to know, too much to remember and too much to do. You're trying to make progress but the information overload has paralyzed you.

"I'm never gonna get over this fear of speaking in public. It's just too much!"

Stop fretting! There is nothing wrong with you. There is a biological, chemical and physical reason your brain does this to you, or perhaps I should say your brain does this *for* you. There's also a way to beat it. The culprit is something called your amygdala.

The amygdala is a section of your brain that developed about 500 million years ago. It is your fight-or-flight mechanism. It protects you from harm.

When you find yourself in a life-or-death situation such as coming upon a bear in the woods, a person threatening you with physical harm or a car coming at yours in the wrong direction your amygdala goes into action and comes to your rescue. Your amygdala goes into fight-or-flight mode and shuts down any brain activity that would interfere with your ability to either run or fight. Rational thinking, creative thinking, digestion, sexual desire and thought processes all get shut down so that your brain is focused only on saving yourself.

The problem is that those same amygdala warning bells go off whenever you try something new. If you step out of your comfort zone and attempt to try something new or to get into a new routine, the amygdala signals danger and shuts most of your brain down. Purposeful action and creativity is suppressed. No wonder you can't get anywhere!

If I may take literary liberty here with an old Tiny Tim song, "let's tiptoe past the amygdala!" Let's not alert it to overwhelm. Let's take small steps. We do this by employing the Chinese technique of *kaizen,* taking small steps to accomplish big things. Dr. Robert Maurer, Ph. D. has written a wonderful book called *One Small Step Can Change Your Life The Kaizen Way* that explains the technique in detail. I highly recommend it. My explanation herein of kaizen is based directly upon Dr. Maurer's book.

To tiptoe past the amygdala to conquer the fear of public speaking we're going to take small steps. When I say small steps I mean *really* small steps. Steps so small as to make you think they are insignificant and will probably have you saying, "Come on, Tom. This is ridiculous!" I understand.

Here we go. Imagine you have to do a speech. Overwhelm and brain paralysis are just around the corner, right? Wait! Try this. Get a notepad and a pen and set them down on your desk, the countertop or perhaps the kitchen table. That's it. You're finished. Do not do anything else! Let the pad and pen just sit there for an hour, a day or even a week. No overwhelm here and the amygdala doesn't notice a thing. But guess what? You've started!

What is the topic of your speech? Can you think of one or two ideas for a title? Good. Write them down on the pad. Done! Don't do anything else. See ya tomorrow. The amygdala remains clueless.

Are there a few main points you want to include in your speech? Write them down. Stop. Now go mow the lawn, do the dishes or clean the house. Your amygdala has no idea what you're up to.

Could you write a line or two or even a paragraph about one of the points you want to make? Maybe you could get really ambitious and even tackle *two* points. Just a couple and call it a day. Shhhh! Your amygdala is still sleeping.

When you come back take a look at the rest of your points and do a few lines or a paragraph about each. Now it's time for your favorite TV show.

Imagine you are about to give your speech. What are the first two or three things you'd like to say to your audience? Perhaps a welcome, then introduce yourself followed by a brief line of what you'll be talking about. Enough already! See, quietly tiptoeing.

How would you like to end your speech? With a story? An example? A reinforcement of the points you made? A call to action? Don't call to loudly because you'll wake up you-know-who.

Through the simplicity and magic of kaizen look at what you have done one small step at a time. "Hmmm" you say. "I've got a pad filled with stuff. I have a title – even two to choose from. I have four main points. I have a paragraph about each point which I could easily expand upon. I have an opening to my speech. I have a close. My goodness, I have a speech!"

Remember, as you complete each small step your confidence will build as you realize you are reaching your goal small step by small step. And through it all, no overwhelm. Your amygdala never knew what happened!

Chapter 14:

Change The Meaning!

Associations are extremely powerful. Remember when I told you about my fear of flying? Well, one of the things I tried was a Fear-of-Flying class. For ten consecutive Saturdays I drove two hours to Milwaukee's Mitchell International Airport where a class was being offered by a psychiatrist who also happened to be a pilot. I reasoned that a psychiatrist who was also a pilot was the can't-miss combination to get me over my fear of flying. Part of what he taught us was the physical aspects of a jet airplane, the mechanics of the aircraft, the aerodynamics, why it flies and how it flies. I took comfort in learning that when a plane is in the sky the air essentially encases the wings as if they were in concrete – the wings can't move and barring human error the plane can't go down.

What I found most interesting however, was what he told all of us at the beginning of the very first class. He said none of us was afraid of an airplane or flying. Our real issue was that in an airplane we have no control over our fate – somebody else is flying the plane and we just have to trust that person to get us safely to our destination. He went on to say our issue with flying is that we associate it with a time in our past – a traumatic incident where we were totally out of control and our fate was in someone else's hands. Our goal in this class, he said, was to go back and resurrect that incident so we could deal with it and erase that association. But he also cautioned that not all of us would be able to reach back into our past to bring out the traumatic incident. As luck would have it, I was one of the cases where it didn't work. I wasn't able to go back and find it. I do have my suspicions as to where my insecurities came from but that's for another book! There were those in the class who successfully went back in time and when they dredged up that past incident it became very obvious through tears and some pretty dramatic emotional displays that they had uncovered the out-of-control painful experience they now associated to flying.

In the case of one young lady, she remembered back to the night she was working at a convenience store and suddenly found herself with a knife being held to her throat. At that moment she had no control over what was to become of her life. It was literally in somebody else's hands.

Another person in the class, a man in his early 50's said he wasn't always afraid to fly. In fact he had done quite a bit of travelling by air. But then came the day that his four-year-old son was choking on a peach pit. The man grabbed his son, pounded him on the back, shook him, turned him upside down and did everything he possibly knew how to do to dislodge the peach pit from his son's throat. None of it worked and the boy died in his father's arms. He had no control over his son's fate. Sometime later the man and his wife booked a flight to Florida and everything was normal on the day of the trip until the man was about to hand his boarding pass to the flight attendant and enter the doorway of the plane. He couldn't. He stopped dead in his tracks and nothing or no one was going to make him budge and cross that line through the plane's doorway. As he explained it to our class the thought of stepping through the doorway triggered the feeling that he would no longer be in control and his fate would be in the hands of the pilot and the flight crew. The association here was obvious. He thought back to that last time he had no control – the event that caused him ultimate pain – the loss of his son.

A postscript to this story: At the end of our ten-week class, the final exam if you will, was to take a flight together as a group with the instructor to St. Louis and back. This one-hour flight would give each of us an indication of how far we had come in dealing with our fear of flying.

The young lady who had the knife held to her throat got in her seat and began to cry but with some words of comfort and encouragement from the instructor who put his arm around her she made it. I am sorry to tell you that the man whose son died in his arms could not get on the plane. He didn't even show up for our flight. To paraphrase our instructor, the man needed more help than what could be accomplished in our ten-week class.

So how does this story relate to the fear of speaking in public? When you think about it, the young lady who experienced the convenience store trauma and the man who lost his son weren't afraid of airplanes, or air or airplane doorways. No. Their fear was the result of a misdirected association. A robbery involving a knife and the loss of a child have nothing to do with flying but these two people made the connection. Even though the association had no basis in fact it was real to them because they made it real in their heads. You know this is true because the people on the flight who were not part of our class had very different, yet very powerful, positive associations to what flying to St. Louis that day meant. To them the association was, "I'll get to see those famous arches in person", "Tonight I'll be at a Cardinals baseball game", "In an hour I'll be greeted by family I haven't seen in a year" or, "This is the business deal I've been working on for weeks and today we finally close it."Same airplane, same flight, same destination but very different associations. For some people the flight was heaven, for others hell.

I'm sure you know by now that I always bring my stories back around to *you* because 'you' is why we're here! My fearful-flyer classmates and I were not afraid of airplanes. You are not afraid of the 'public' are you? If you were you'd never be able to go to the grocery store, the bank, Walmart or a restaurant. You're certainly not afraid of 'speaking' are you? You do it all day everyday. You're not afraid of your job – you know it inside and out. And you're certainly not afraid of a hotel or conference center ballroom – you've been in many of them for anything from meetings to weddings.Yet, when you put all those things you're *not* afraid of together – speaking, the public, your job and a ballroom, *you're pushing the panic button*! You see, just like those fearful flyers, it's the association you make that makes all the difference.

So, let's come up with some new associations about speaking in public. You gotta tell yourself a different story about what speaking in public means to you. Nothing has any meaning except the meaning you give to it. You may believe that the meaning you attach to a certain event or situation is absolutely correct, accurate and irrefutable. Yet, to another person, that same event or situation has a totally opposite meaning or means nothing at all!

Chapter 15:

Mississippi Queen

Could you possibly imagine the overwhelming excitement of meeting Leslie West? If I met him I would first tremble, then perhaps faint and when I woke up I'd give myself permission to die because my life would be complete!

But wait! You're reading this asking, "Leslie who?" Leslie West is the lead guitarist for the late-60's-early-70's rock band *Mountain*. The only way you would possibly know who Mountain was is to tell you they had a 70's hit record called *Mississippi Queen*. I have idolized Leslie West and Mountain for more than 46 years. Leslie West and Mountain are so deeply ingrained into the fabric of my life that my son is under orders to play two particular Mountain songs at my funeral service!

Yet, if you met Leslie West it would mean *absolutely nothing to you.*

Nothing and no one has any meaning except the meaning *you* give it. Like your audience and public speaking, maybe?

***Nothing has any meaning except
the meaning you give to it.***

Chapter 16:

Believe You Are Unstoppable!

Beliefs are powerful. If you believe something strongly enough it will eventually become your reality. After all, a belief is simply something you've told yourself over and over again until it became true in your own mind.

Here is a mind game you can use to make yourself believe that you are a force to be reckoned with when it comes to public speaking. This technique may sound somewhat egotistical and it's something you would never say to anyone else or in public. But when you say it to yourself over and over again you'll start to feel it and believe it. Here is all you need to say to yourself as you imagine yourself getting up to speak before a group (feel free to use your own variation if you'd like). "There's a reason *I'm* up here and *you're* not. *I* have the information *you* need. This is *my* room. *I* own it. *I'm* in charge. You all *wish* you had the nerve to get up here and do what I'm doing. You don't."

Sounds egotistical, doesn't it? That's ok. Because while I might agree with you that it sounds egotistical there's something else you should know about the mantra – it's absolutely true! Let's break it down.

There definitely is a reason *you're* up there and *they're* not. The person who asked you to give the speech or presentation saw something in you that they didn't see in your colleagues. The person who asked you to do the presentation was convinced you had a better grasp of the information than anyone else. As a result of those two things being true, it *is* your room, you *do* own it and you *are* in charge! And truth be told, the other people in the room wouldn't have it any other way!

If you *believe* our egotistical mantra then you will *act* that way. If you act that way your audience will believe it. Remember, perception is reality. If your audience believes you're a confident, in-charge, commanding speaker – you are! Remember, people will believe what you show yourself to be.

A little attitude and anger never hurt, either!

Although we don't fully understand the power of ego, it definitely has power. Don't underestimate it. Accept the accolades and feed your ego with them. Your self-esteem will begin to build.

Chapter 17:

Disaster And Diets

What did September 11, 2001 mean to you when the airplanes hit the Twin Towers of New York's World Trade Center killing almost 3000 people? For some it meant terrorists had gained a foothold in the U.S. and more death and destruction was sure to follow. To others it meant a wakeup call, renewed patriotism and a pledge to be vigilant so that it would never happen again. What about going on a diet? Boy, there's one that brings about two very different and opposite meanings. To some it means "depriving myself of all the stuff I love. No more snacks and junk food while I'm watching TV.What's the point of living if you can't have a greasy cheeseburger, enchiladas or deep-fried anything?" For others going on a diet means healthier eating, fresh foods, lower blood pressure, lower cholesterol, breathing better, sleeping better and more energy – not to mention looking better. You see, one person's pain is another's pleasure. It's all in what you associate to it.

A great way to change your negative association or negative meaning to anything is to ask the question, "What's good about this?" That's precisely what we just did with the examples of September 11 and dieting. By asking the question "What's good about this?" you give the situation a new, more empowering meaning. September 11 could be viewed as the day America began to live in fear or as the day the terrorists awakened a sleeping giant. One can view dieting as either "all the vices and pleasures I'll have to live without" or "all the things I'll gain."

So let me ask you what you associate public speaking to. Probably pain, right? "My voice isn't good enough." "I don't look good enough." "They're going to criticize me." "They're going to know that I'm nervous." "They know the subject better than I do." If those are the associations you're making who could blame you for not wanting to give a speech? In your mind, getting up in front of an audience and giving a speech equals pain!

What would happen if you changed that association? What if you started telling your subconscious a different story? What if you uninstalled your old way of thinking about public speaking and instead installed a thinking pattern that made you associate public speaking with pleasure. What are some of the things you could say to yourself to turn pain to pleasure and maybe even into power?

It's time to link pleasure to the words "Why me?" You're very familiar with the words "Why me?" aren't you. It's what you say to yourself after your boss or your organization asks you to give a presentation. "Why me?" right? "There are so many other people who could do it!"

"Life begins at the end of your comfort zone."
Neale Donald Walsch
Author 'Conversations With God' series

Let me give you an example from my own life of something that has no doubt happened in your family, too. My

66

brother John was getting married and he needed someone to serve as his best man. At most weddings the best man's responsibilities include giving a speech at the rehearsal dinner and to propose a toast at the wedding reception the next day. John narrowed his best man choices down to three – brother Josh, brother Matthew or me. He chose Josh. In most families when one brother asks another to be his best man there are tears, loud back slaps, big bear hugs and "Oh, gumba, what an honor!" Not in my family! When John chose Josh, Josh's immediate reaction was, "Oh, darn it John. Whydya hafta pick me? You coulda chose Matt, you coulda chose Tom – so why the heck did you have to pick me?" And if the truth be told, he used words other than "darn it" and "why the heck" if you know what I mean. To Josh, being asked to be best man meant pain! He had to give not one speech, but two. He'd have to think of some flowery, sappy words to say for the toast and he'd have to do it in front of not only strangers but also before every member of his family which can sometimes be *worse* than performing for strangers.

Did John choose Josh to inflict pain on his brother or to make his brother's life miserable? No. What was the real meaning behind John's choice? What new meaning could Josh have given it? What could Josh have said to himself so that he would link pleasure to John's request? He could have started with, "Hmmm, I must be special. Why did he choose me? Matt's a technician for a major oil company and Tom is a television news anchor – they're no dummies. And John loves all of his brothers the same but he picked me to play a major role in the most important day of his life. He obviously thinks I can do it otherwise he wouldn't have picked me for this big day."

Josh could have also linked pleasure to the process and the aftermath as well. What could be more fun than sitting at the kitchen table mapping out a speech where you get to dredge up stories about John, tell a few tales out of school, make John squirm a bit, get a few laughs and then wrap it up with how happy everyone is for John and his new bride. The pleasure of the aftermath would be the compliments Josh would be sure to receive not just at the reception following his speech but for days, weeks and even months later as everyone reminisces about the day and comments on what a great job Josh did to make the day even more special. Now that's pleasure. Will there be a little bit of pain involved for Josh? Certainly! I don't know anyone who is absolutely thrilled at the prospect of giving the wedding speech and toast. You're on the hot seat and you want to make it good so yes, there's more than just a little bit of anxiety involved. But compare that little bit of anxiety to the reward at the end and it's more than worth it.

By the way, Josh was great.

So let's bring this around to you and the speech you have to give. "Why me?" you say. Well, here's why. There was probably a meeting of the powers-that-be at your company or at an organization you belong to and they needed a speaker for a convention or to make a presentation to prospective clients. Isn't it funny how they chose *you* over anyone else? Did they do it to punish you? Did they do it because they thought you were a great guy? No and no. The only reason that you were chosen is that the higher-ups are convinced that your performance will reflect well on the company or organization. It enhances the company's stature and image and the end result will be an increase in sales of whatever product your company is involved in. Your expertise and knowledge lends credibility to your company which translates to sales, money and an improved bottom line. So link pleasure to being asked to give a presentation because the *bottom line* is they think you're good for the *bottom line*!

This doesn't just apply to business. You're probably involved in one or more service organizations – it could be Rotary, the Lions Club, Kiwanis, Mensa or you may sit on the board of your local American Cancer Society, American Heart Association, Muscular Distrophy Association or any number of other organizations. When your organization asks you to make a presentation it's because they believe your knowledge of the organization, your involvement, your compassion, your drive and your personality will translate into a successful fundraising effort or elevate the organization's image before the general public. Again, just like in business, they want you there because you're good. And isn't it always pleasurable when someone tells you you're good?

You might now be asking, understandably, "If this presentation is so important to the company's image, credibility, sales or fundraising why doesn't the *boss* do it?" Aha! Yet another way for you to link pleasure to public speaking! Why doesn't the boss do it? Simple. He doesn't know as much as you do, that's why!I don't mean to disparage bosses but the boss's job is to be the boss, to manage talented people and to see that those talents are best used to enhance the company's bottom line. Examples of what I'm saying are everywhere. Can the manager of the winning team in the World Series hit a 90-mile-per-hour fastball? I doubt that he'd even *see* the ball coming at him at that speed! Can the head coach of the winning team in the Super Bowl take a handoff and rush for 10 yards? Not without getting killed! My own boss who is my television station's news director is a wonderful administrator and manager of people. But guess what would happen if he ever tried to anchor the 6 o'clock news? Viewers would run for their remotes and advertisers would run for other television stations! Baseball players know how to hit, NFL running backs know how to run, TV news anchors know how to anchor and managers know how to manage. I had a television station general manager who made this point very well. He said, "I like being the 'general' manager." He wasn't saying 'general' in a military sense like "I like being the general." No, he was saying it more in terms of being the jack of all trades and master of none. He was essentially saying, "I may be the head of this company but I can't do what my employees can do." He certainly didn't know the engineering and electronic intricacies of a television station, especially in this day of satellite and digital technology. He couldn't run the accounting department or business office, write commercial copy, anchor, produce, shoot video or maintain the computer system – all things absolutely necessary for the successful operation of a television station. He can't do any of it, and yet, he's the boss. His job is to make sure all of those departments are performing at their peak to insure a bigger bottom line. Jack of all trades, master of none. That's why you're giving the speech or presentation and not the boss. Link it up. Pleasure.

Lets link up more pleasure. When the higher-ups ask you to do a speech or presentation they are essentially telling you, "No one knows this stuff like you do, certainly not us so there's no one better than you to make this company look good." By the way, this also leads to some nice perks like road trips. The higher-ups say, "Man if he's this good let's get him out on the road face-to-face with our customers and clients." That certainly doesn't hurt your prospects for promotions and raises. In this day and age of job insecurity that's got to feel good and pleasurable.

Chapter 18:

Six Figures Or Eight Figures? Speaking Figures!

Did you know that your ability to speak in public can accelerate your career? I don't mean it can result in some minor promotion or a meager pay raise. No, I'm talking Acceleration with a capital 'A' as in accelerating your career by five and even as much as ten years!

Just think of what that would mean in real dollars and cents. Come up with your best estimate of what your weekly income will be ten years from today. Now imagine making that kind of money right now. *Today!*

Communication skills are invaluable and companies will reward the person who has that ability. Every business or organization needs a confident, well-versed spokesperson to be its public face.

My locker at the YMCA was next to the locker of the CEO of a multi-billion dollar worldwide corporation. He had been with the company for nearly 30 years and worked his way up through the ranks until he finally made it to the top with the corner office andthe mahogany desk. His annual compensation was in the millions of dollars.

One day after a workout he and I were chatting about his upcoming retirement. I half-jokingly said, "Boy, that salary's gotta be hard to walk away from!" His response was, "Oh, the salary's not the big thing. I've got $40 million in stock options."

I do not tell you this story to impress you with the fact that a multi-millionaire had a locker next to mine. No, the real story is that months later I was talking with someone who was a member of this corporation's board of directors and who was familiar with my CEO friend's climb to the top. To my surprise I learned that my CEO friend almost didn't get the job!

It seems that while the board was impressed with my friend's leadership skills, salesmanship and business savvy, they found him to be lacking in one important area – public speaking and that made them hesitate to pull the trigger on his coronation as CEO. They were able to gently suggest to him that he seek help in improving this weakness. He did and soon after that the board of directors voted to name him the company's new CEO.

Before he got to the top my friend was making a respectable six-figure income. Because of his willingness to improve his public speaking skills he turned six-figures into seven with $40 million in stock options thrown in for good measure upon his retirement.

The ability to speak publicly could accelerate your career by five and even ten years!
Think about it!

Chapter 19:

A Tool For Good Or Evil

To see just how powerful the ability to speak publicly is, one need only look to history. Throughout time there have been famous examples of how speech was used as a unifying force and also as a weapon of verbal mass destruction.

President Ronald Reagan pressured an oppressive Communist government into action with the words, "Mr. Gorbachev, tear down this wall." President Franklin D. Roosevelt changed our nation's psyche with the words, "The only thing we have to fear is fear itself." Dr. Martin Luther King inspired a nation to look at itself with the words, "I have a dream."

There are other, not so noble examples of the power of speech. Charles Manson used the power to move his followers to murder. People's Temple leader Jim Jones convinced more than 900 people at a compound in Guyana to commit mass suicide. Adolph Hitler used the power to murder 6 million people in the name of a superior race.

You may not be a world leader and you certainly are not an historical despot. However, you do have something in common with all of them – the power you wield when you have the ability to speak.

Chapter 20:

Know Thine Audience

In this next section on dealing with the mental aspect of public speaking I want to spend some time on your audience. Perhaps I should say your *audiences* – plural. There are two – the audience you *think* is out there and the audience that's *actually* out there. They are two very different audiences and I think when you see the difference you'll have a whole lot more confidence the next time you give a speech or make a presentation.

So just who is out there? Typically, they are your co-workers, peers, friends and business associates who you have no trouble talking to every day. But as soon as they take their seats in the meeting room or the convention hall they turn into your worst nightmare! They become vampires, the Big Bad Wolf, the neighbor's pit bull and your mother-in-law all rolled into one and they're out to get you, right? You are absolutely convinced they're looking for any little flaw they can attack you on. All they need to see is just a little blood in the water and like sharks they'll eat you alive. You say to yourself, "They're staring at me, they're criticizing the way I'm dressed, I've got a terrible voice, what if they think I don't know my stuff, what if I embarrass myself?" In reality, there is just one person in the room thinking those things – you! You have been building up this scenario in your head for days, maybe even weeks before you had to do the presentation. Isn't it funny the tricks our brains can play on us when we're dealing with the unknown?

How many times have you fretted, lost sleep, even became ill over something you had to do and then when you finally did it, it was nothing and you kicked yourself for the unnecessary hell you put yourself through? There is a saying that goes, "A coward dies a thousand deaths, a courageous man but once." It's happened to all of us at least once, if not one hundred times. Think back to that colonoscopy, vasectomy or mammogram. Remember the horror stories you heard from other people who had those procedures done? You were ready to cancel the appointment. But you went through with it and when it was over you said, "Is that it? *That's* what everybody thought was so horrible? That was nothing."

I will admit it still happens to me. Here's proof!

Chapter 21:

"Tom, The Colonel Is Here."

I had the privilege of emceeing a big military veterans event to honor women in the military. As part of my duties that day I would not only introduce fourteen women soldiers to the crowd of one thousand people but I would also introduce the day's guest speaker – a full-fledged colonel. This colonel also happened to be the highest-ranking member of the state's Desert Veterans organization. This colonel had served in Operation Desert Storm and Desert Shield as well as at the Pentagon. For weeks prior to the event I had thoughts like, "How do I dress? What do I say? I gotta make sure I position the microphone on the podium so that the medals on the colonel's chest don't clang and make noise."

The big day arrived and as I stood offstage going over my emcee script while hundreds of people milled about, one of the event's organizers came up to me and said, "Tom, the colonel is here." Oh boy, here we go. I dutifully followed the event organizer through the crowd and then we stopped. The event organizer said, "Tom, I'd like you to meet Colonel Christiansen." I found myself face-to-face with a woman in her 60's, about 5-foot-2, wearing khaki pants and a University of Wisconsin Badgers sweatshirt. She extended her hand to me and said, "Hi, Tom. Marge Christiansen." You could have knocked me over with a feather! Marge Christiansen. Colonel Margaret Christiansen – the colonel I had fretted about meeting for weeks!

The point of the story is that we let things build up in our heads and we imagine the worst. So let's all stop doing that!

You've built up your audience to be 'The Colonel'. They're just 'Marge'.

You are already off to a good start. Remember, nothing ever gets better until you admit that something is wrong and you've admitted *something* is wrong! You've told yourself that you don't have what it takes to get up in front of an audience, but deep down inside you know that's not true. You have also convinced yourself that your audience is out to get you but deep down inside you know that's not true either. How do *I* know that *you* know these things are not true? Because you're here! You took action and you either went to the bookstore or online and you bought this book! If you *really* thought you didn't have what it takes and if you *really* thought that your audience is out to get you, you wouldn't be here right now. You'd have given up. Deep down inside you know that your fear is F.E.A.R – False Evidence Appearing Real. You are not willing to accept your current way of thinking about public speaking. There is an angry, determined voice inside of you saying, "If they can do it, I can do it." The key is to just start. It doesn't matter if you start wrong, just start. If you begin a trip by getting on the wrong highway you'll soon figure out you're off course, you'll make corrections and eventually arrive at your destination. Even if it's a wrong start, just start.

Chapter 22:

A 'Rocky' Start

My first guitar lesson at the age of 14 is a perfect example of someone starting *completely* wrong yet ending up with complete success. I was so excited on the day of that first Saturday lesson. I arrived at the music store where the teacher was waiting for me, took my guitar out of its case, sat down in a chair, rested the guitar in my lap and I was all set for the teacher to show me how to play that thing. Of course, I thought the teacher would start by telling me how great it was that I was learning to play the guitar and about all the joy it would bring me throughout my life. Instead, my teacher, Rocky Stranieri looked at me and said, "What are you doing?"I said, "What do you mean?" He said, "You got the guitar upside down and you've got the pick in the wrong hand. You gotta flip the guitar around so that the neck sticks out the other way and you've gotta put the pick in your other hand."My response to him was, "But I gotta play it this way – I'm left-handed."He said, "Oh, so you're a left-handed guitar player, are you? How long you been playin' guitar?" I said, "I've never played. That's why I'm here. This is my first lesson." And he said, "So, you're not a left-handed guitarist and you're not a right-handed guitarist because you're not a guitarist at all! And since right now you can't play left-handed or right-handed, you could learn either way. And since you have a right-handed guitar, you're going to be a right-handed guitar player!"

Point of the story – I started out my thinking about playing guitar all wrong. Somebody showed me the right way and now, all these years later while I am not a rock star I can play the instrument and I truly enjoy it. And it all started out with me being wrong. Yeah, the guitar was upside down but what was most important is that I had the guitar in my lap and I was ready to learn. Kind of like certain people's upside down view of their capabilities and their audience! Recognize anybody? Like, you?

So here *you* are, ready to learn how to get over the fear of speaking in public and you're starting all wrong with the wrong idea of who your audience is. So let's get this guitar flipped around right now! And the way we're going to do it is by realizing who your audience really *is* and *is not* and maybe even more important – who your audience *thinks* you are!

You might look at it this way -- who your audience *thinks* you are is who *you tell them and show them* you are. Your words, your demeanor, the way you dress and the way you carry yourself all send signals to the audience about who you are and how you are to be perceived. This is a great trick and it works because *you* don't have to believe it, you just gotta make sure *they* believe it!

I learned just how true this is when I was about 10 years old. This was somewhere around 1962. My father was a school teacher making just above poverty-level wages so he certainly wasn't influential, wealthy or "somebody." After a day of teaching at the high school he picked me up from grade school and we had to stop at the Finast grocery store to pick up a few things. Once inside the store we both *had to go*! We really needed the men's room – but back in those days there were no public restrooms for customers – no big sign that said

79

Restrooms – just bathrooms way in the back room for employees, that's all.

Well, my dad, dressed in his suit and tie said, "Come, follow me." My dad put his hands in his pockets and strutted past the meat counter as though he owned the place. The employees apparently thought he really did own the place because as we walked past them they nodded their heads respectfully, they said "Hello sir" and when my father asked, "Where's the bathroom?" the employees respectfully responded, "Through those double doors, sir". Those double doors were those swinging double doors you find at the back corner of every grocery store – the double doors that lead into the back stock room where all the stuff comes out of to be put on the shelves. We pushed through the double doors and we encountered more employees, all of whom nodded respectfully and called my dad, "sir".

We used the facility, did our shopping and left the store. I left with a lesson. You are who your audience *thinks* you are. You are who you *tell* your audience you are. I am sure those grocery store employees were absolutely convinced that on that day they had come face-to-face with the CEO!

"If ya got it and ya know ya got it, ya got it.
If ya got it but you don't know ya got it,
ya don't got it.
If ya don't got it but ya think ya got it, ya got it."
Jackie Gleason

Chapter 23:

Oh My God, You Scared Me!

I always notice something interesting when a corporation or company asks me to come in and conduct a seminar to help their employees or management team with speaking issues. I'll begin by asking some of the attendees a few questions about their fear of speaking in public. "What makes you nervous? What makes you uncomfortable? Where does this fear come from?" The answer is usually, "I'm afraid of being in front of an audience." So I'll ask, "Who's your audience?" And the person will say, "The people I work with."I'll respond with, "Oh, *these* people. The same people you have lunch with, gossip with, talk with, work with all day – your extended family. *These* people?" At that point everyone starts to laugh and then I'll ask the next person, "What are you afraid of?" And I get the same answer, *these people*. Until finally, the whole room realizes the absurdity of *everybody* in the room being afraid of *everybody* in the room – their friends, co-workers, co-gossipers, co-lunch mates and extended family!

Another example of how we're afraid of each other happens somewhere it should *never* happen – church! Sunday services! I don't know what religion you practice or if you even have a religion, but I happen to have been raised in the Catholic church and if you're a Catholic or have ever had occasion to attend a Catholic service then you know there comes a point in the mass where the priest asks everyone to join hands as the congregation recites The Lord's Prayer. Now, I get the intent of the gesture, but let's be honest. Nobody likes it. First, ya gotta hold hands with a stranger. Second, the stranger's hands are either cold, sweaty or clammy. And they're thinking the same thing about you! Or you wind up joining hands with an 8-year-old who's wondering, "Who is this guy?" And worst of all, if you're a guy, you sometimes wind up holding another guy's hand! I'm sorry, but I feel no Divine Intervention at that point. All I'm waiting for is the last line of the prayer, "...and lead us not into temptation but deliver us from evil, amen." All I'm thinking is, "deliver me from this guy's hand, amen!"

A similar thing happens later in that same service when everyone is invited to extend the sign of peace to each other. You're supposed to shake hands with the person to your left, your right as well as the person in front of and behind you along with whoever you can reach and whoever can reach you. As you shake hands you're supposed to say, "Peace be with you." This is church so let me make a confession. I hate this and I can't wait for this 30 seconds of handshaking and peace offering to end! Of *course* I wish you all peace, but my handshake is not going to bring you peace. I don't even know you. You know what I get out of this? When I turn around to extend my hand I get to say to myself, "Oh, you're the guy who's been snoring!"

Chapter 24:

Dyadic Transactional Communication

Oh, don't we sound just so sophisticated now?

When I was working toward a Masters Degree in Speech I took a high-and-mighty- sounding course called Dyadic Transactional Communication. Dyadic transactional communication can be explained in five simple words, "I see you seeing me." That's what dyadic transactional communication is – two people (a dyad) interacting with each other and reacting to what the other just said or did. You, me and everyone you know did this all night long on our first date as we nervously and awkwardly responded to and reacted to what the other person was saying and doing! Now I'll bet you understand!

So, you ask, "What the heck does dyadic transactional communication have to do with getting me over my fear of public speaking?" Dyadic transactional communication is the basis of your fear. You see your audience seeing you. You think you know what they're thinking about you and you react to that belief. But what if what you thought they were thinking was completely wrong? What if they were thinking just the opposite of what you *thought* they were thinking? How would that change your reaction and how you felt about yourself?

Take a look at these two lists and I think you'll see what I mean. First, how *you* perceive your audience:

THEY WANT TO SEE ME FAIL. I JUST KNOW IT!

1. They're staring at me.

2. They're criticizing the way I'm dressed.

3. They think I have a terrible voice.

4. They think I don't know my stuff.

5. They're waiting for me to embarrass myself.

If you thought this is what your audience was thinking then your fear would be completely understandable. How can you have any degree of confidence if you think your audience sees blood in the water? But what if your perception of what they're thinking is wrong? What if they're thinking just the opposite? Then how would you react? Then how would you feel about yourself?

WHAT THEY'RE *REALLY* THINKING

1. How does he have the guts to get up and do that?

2. Where did he learn to give speeches like that?

3. I wouldn't know half that stuff.

4. Damn, I'm jealous. I'd never be able to do that.

5. I am *so* glad I'm not the one who's up there.

The only power your audience has over you is the power you give them. Don't give them the power. They are not stopping you from doing anything. Instead, feed your courage with your audience's insecurity. They see you as someone who is better than they are. They see you as an authority and someone who is to be looked up to and respected.

When you have finished your presentation, your audience will ask, "Who was that?" "Was that really you?" You will be a different person in their eyes.

OK, let's lighten things up a little bit. Here's how the audience really sees you. They already love you because you gave them a break from a mundane day at the office. They get coffee and pastry and don't have to do a thing because you're doing all the work. They just have to sit there and clap. It's a friendly audience already on your side. They are your co-workers. They are your friends. They know how it would feel if they had to do it.

Always remember that for the most part the audience is made up of your friends. They are nice people. They want to see you succeed. Take every opportunity to communicate with them. Communicate to them how good *they* are. Communicate to them how good *you* are.

Chapter 25:

The Finish Line – Let's Get Physical!

Failure is a trickster with a keen sense of irony and cunning. It takes great delight in tripping one when success is almost within reach. Napolean Hill 'Think And Grow Rich'

Welcome to the third and final leg of our journey on the road to beating the fear of public speaking. First, let me congratulate you. You got through the hard stuff and I know it wasn't easy. You confronted your fear head-on and that wasn't fun, was it? You came face-to-face with the emotional and mental aspects of getting over your anxiety. Kind of a rude awakening, wasn't it? It's not very pleasant when someone – namely me – first tells you the emotions you associate to public speaking are all irrational. Then I told you those fears were put in your head as a child by people who loved you and wanted the best for you and wanted to protect you. And finally, I told you you've been afraid of a ghost that never existed. It's almost like somebody politely telling you you're crazy, right?

Then to add insult to injury I told you that everything you've ever thought about your audience, how they perceive you and what they think of you is wrong. OK, at this point I would understand if you were saying. "Oh great, Tom. Some supportive coach *you* are!"

Call it tough love, but give yourself a pat on the back because you were tougher. You listened. You learned. You thought about it and decided to continue anyway despite what this Zalaski guy was throwing at you!

So thanks for stickin' with me. It'll be worth it, I promise you.

We now come to the third element of our journey, the physical. And I gotta tell you this is the part of the program I am most excited about. Yes, the emotional segment was important and so was the mental. But the reason I like the physical best is because it's what you have the most immediate control over. And if you take care of the physical, handling the emotional and the mental will be much easier.

It won't be fear that ruins your speech. It will be logistics. Something at the venue that you did not expect and had no control over. Somebody else screwed up, not you. So our job is to minimize that risk. Let's lay out what could go wrong and make sure it goes right.

> *"This is my show. I want no surprises.*
> *I will leave nothing to chance."*
> ***Adopt This Attitude***

So what do I mean when I say physical? I mean everything you are going to do, see, feel, smell and experience on the day of your speech. At this point you might be saying,

"Oh great Tom, you're going to tell me what it's going to feel like on the day of my speech." Or, "Great Tom – you have anchored 50,000 newscasts and appeared before countless crowds and now you're going to tell me what it's going to feel like and how simple it's going to be. Really?"No! I hope you know by now you can expect more from me than that and I demand nothing less of myself than giving you ten times what I promise!

Not only are you going to do your speech – sometimes *at* the venue *before* the actual day but I'm also going to arm you with all of the information you'll need about anything that could go wrong and how to make sure it doesn't.My friend, this is the formula I use for my own speeches and appearances so I'm not going to give you some hypothetical scenario. I'm going to give you my routine and it's a can't-fail routine and the reason it's a can't-fail routine is because this is my life and my living – so if for no other reason than my own self-interest, it had better work, right? This is exactly what I do. As I said before, this is one-stop shopping. I know other programs, websites and videos that you've seen tease you. They give you a little information, get you all excited, make you watch their 'free' video and then they hit you with, "All you have to do is buy this, or sign up for this service, or pay to get in on this webinar", right?

Not this program. You get it all – now! One stop shopping.

Chapter 26:

The Script

OK, you're going to do a speech. If it's your first speech our goal is to get you on and off stage with a respectable performance in between. That's all. This is not the time to teach you the intricacies of a *great* speech. This is not the time to delve into how to present an attention-grabbing opening line or a hard-hitting, effective closing line. We'll leave that stuff to the university speech teachers, the so-called speech 'coaches' or the slick sales pitch guys. For those of you who have done two or three speeches our goal is to get you to that next step.

The most obvious, logical first step is to *write your speech*! This should be easy now that you know the kaizen technique! As you do keep in mind that while 12-point font or type works well when you're reading and rehearsing in the comfort of your kitchen, 12-point type doesn't work very well at a podium. Your script will be sitting on a podium 2 feet away from your face, a microphone is between your eyes and the paper and the lighting isn't quite what it was in your kitchen. To make matters worse, your 12-point type is probably single-spaced, right?

So let's get around the trouble spots. Here are my tips for the perfect, can't fail script.

- Type your script in 18-point font (16-point if your eyesight is really good!) It *got* to be easily readable!

- Double space it (or at least one-and-a-half spaces)

- Be sure the last paragraph or sentence on a page does not run onto the next page. Turning the page to get to the rest of the sentence or paragraph may make you lose your cadence or even your train of thought.

- Practice turning the pages. Seriously! We've all run into the problem of trying to turn a page in a book or a document and the page just didn't want to turn! The pages stuck together. Your fingers were dry and you couldn't turn one page to get to the next one, right? Early in my career I learned the hard way that I had this dry finger problem. Unfortunately for me I learned I had the problem while I was on live TV! Talk about a frighteningly rude awakening! After I got off the air the first thing I tried was to put hand lotion on my hands hoping to make my fingers moist and sticky enough so that I could turn the pages. Well, all that did was help the pages stick together even more and I made a sticky mess in the process. It smelled good but it was a mess! The solution I finally found that I've been using for more than 30 years now – I physically crumple or wrinkle the right side of each page at about the middle of the page. That way I've got something to grab on to as I turn the page. My script looks like the dog got hold of it but hey, it works for me and that's all that counts. So devise your own system and practice it *before* you're up at the podium!

- Make two copies of your speech, better yet, three! One copy is the one you hang on to for dear life on the day of your speech. You will probably have it in a manila folder or some sort of notebook. Worst case scenario – you are going to give your speech at a breakfast meeting and the morning begins with small talk, handshaking, coffee and pastry and at some point you found it necessary to lay your speech down. Suddenly, panic! You realize you laid it down and you forgot to pick it up again. Yes, you'll probably find it but those moments of panic are almost as bad as when you lost track of your child at the beach. So, we need a backup plan or two. Put a second copy of your speech in your purse or under your chair or at your table place setting. And just to be absolutely protected, I leave a third copy in my car so that if somehow the unthinkable happened to my first two copies, I can always send someone out to the car. Now, if you lost your car keys, well all I can say is it just wasn't your day!

There is one more minefield I want to warn you of when it comes to your script. Do *not* put your script on the podium ahead of time! I give you this warning because of a painful and panicked experience I had. I was emceeing an event and before things got started I placed my script on the podium as I attended to other issues.

Once the program began, I introduced the morning's speaker who came to the podium with her speech in hand. However, when she left the podium, she picked up her speech and *my script*! As I retook the podium to introduce the next speaker I made the horrific discovery that my script was gone!

Chapter 27:

Your Best Friend

As soon as you know *where* you'll be doing your presentation I like you to do something you really *don't have to do*! Chalk it up to me being overly protective of you. Call Your Best Friend. I want you to 'experience' the room before the day of your presentation.

Whether your presentation is at a hotel ballroom, a convention hall, an auditorium or just in a conference room where you work, your best first step is to get in touch with your best friend, the person I call the Stage Manager. The Stage Manager is the person in charge of the audio and/or visual department of a particular venue. This is the person who is in charge of the microphones, the sound system, the podium, the lights and the stage. The Stage Manager is your best friend!

A simple telephone call to the hotel or convention center sales or event coordinator is a good first step in connecting with the Stage Manager. I'll call this person SM from this point on.

The SM takes great pride in making sure your event and speech goes off without a hitch. If it's a fancy gala dinner, SM wants to set the perfect mood for cocktail hour with the right music and lighting. SM also wants to make sure all of the evening's speeches, presentations and videos come off flawlessly. Bottom line, if the audience or attendees see it, feel it or hear it, SM takes it as their personal responsibility and domain.

How do I know this? Because I work with SMs all the time. They are true professionals, they take great pride in what they do, they are the nicest people on the planet and nothing makes them happier than making you look good. And there's another reason the SM wants you and your event to look good. It's good business! If your company books a certain convention center, ballroom or hotel conference center for a major event such as a stockholders meeting, a sales presentation, seminar or Christmas party – and when that event goes off like clockwork – you can bet your company is going to book the place for next year's event.

But let's not worry about the big, multi-million dollar conventions. Let's get back to you and the SM. Because for most SM's I know, your *personal* success is every bit as important to them as any large convention.

Now, knowing SMs as I do, they'll be flattered that you called. I don't want to put words in your mouth but when you call, here is essentially what you might want to say – "Hi Bill, my name is Leslie East and I'm with the Nantucket Foods Group. We've booked our company's (annual meeting, stockholders meeting, seminar, convention or party) at your (hotel, convention center or ballroom) and I'll be making a presentation during the event. Bill, I'm just a little concerned about my presentation because I'm not a professional speaker and I don't do this very often so I'm calling to ask if there would be a convenient time for me to meet with you so you could show me the podium I'll be using, the microphones, the lights and the stage. I'd just like to get an idea of what it will be like on the day of the presentation."

I can pretty much guarantee you Bill will be more than happy to meet with you. Now this is great if your event is close to home and you've got weeks to prepare. But some of you might be saying, "Great idea, Tom, but our convention is in Las Vegas and I'm not getting there until the day before it starts." That's OK. If you can meet with Bill the night before or even the morning of for even 5 minutes you'll be much further ahead. You'll have a pretty good idea of what things will be like when you actually do your presentation. You won't be going in cold or blind.

OK, so you've met with Bill and you now have seen the lay of the land and you know what it will be like when you make your presentation. You have just put yourself so far ahead of the game you wouldn't believe it!

Again, this is not a step you absolutely must take. But at the very least, on the day of your presentation, arrive early and go stand behind the podium for a minute, see the microphone, look at where you will lay your script and see what kind of lighting situation you'll be working under. Then, when you actually do your presentation you'll have a certain degree of comfort. You brain will say, "Hey, I've been here before. I know what to expect. This is gonna be ok."

Chapter 28:

Tips That Could Save Your Life!

(Well, at least your speech)

1. Kleenex is your friend! Have some handy either in an easily reachable pocket or tucked into your sleeve. When you are two inches away from a live microphone there is no way to muffle the sniffles!

2. Be mindful of your liquid intake (and I don't necessarily mean alcohol!) Whether it's water, soda pop, iced tea or coffee, cut yourself off as the time for your presentation approaches. Leave ample time to answer nature's call before you are called to the podium. Also remember, nervousness can sometimes compound the urge.

3. Avoid carbonated beverages. My 37 years of doing live television and public speeches has taught me that a carbonated beverage and a live microphone is a deadly combination! Need I say more?

4. The only reason you should ever have a cell phone with you at the podium is to use it as a clock to make sure your speech is within the allotted time. Remember to put it on silent mode ahead of time!

5. Know where the restrooms are.

6. Plan your route from your table to the podium.

7. If you are prone to coughing spells or dry throat it might be a good idea to have a glass of water with you at the podium.

8. Be mindful of what's on the menu if you're doing a dinner speech. You might not want to have that piece of steak , roast beef or chicken. You can't brush your teeth!A piece of meat stuck between your teeth (especially if you wear dentures) can be distracting when you're trying to deliver a speech.Play this one by ear – or tooth!

9. The best ad-libs are written.

10. Jokes can make or break your speech. If you are not a comedian I suggest that you not venture into those waters.

11. Arrive early. Be the first one there. As you are alone, experience the silence and emptiness of the room. Get to know the place. Watch the room gradually fill with people rather than walking in to the overwhelming sight of a room filled to capacity.

Chapter 29:

Rehearse

The more you're prepared, the less you're scared!

It would be wonderful if you could rehearse your presentation at the venue where you will be delivering it. I know that sometimes that's not possible. Your convention, meeting or event might be in another city and access to the venue ahead of time is out of the question. If you don't have the luxury of access to the venue to rehearse, go to Plan B – rehearsing either at home or at the office.

I am a big proponent of rehearsal because it is the key to success in almost any profession. Why do professional football teams watch video of their next opponent? Because it's as if they're really playing against the opponent only in this case it's mentally and not physically. When game day actually arrives, the players feel as though they've "been there, done that."

Hospitals regularly conduct mock disasters and triage drills. If and when the real thing happens, they've "been there, done that."

Fire departments practice ice rescues and even set fire to abandoned buildings to rehearse for the real thing.

The one rehearsal scenario that most of us can identify with is the wedding rehearsal! If you've ever gotten married or were ever in a wedding then you know that without the rehearsal the wedding would have been a disaster!

We go to the batting cages in preparation for softball season. We work certain muscles at the YMCA to get our golf swing ready. We jog in preparation for an upcoming marathon and kids rehearse the school play.

In each case, when the real thing presents itself, the professionals in all of these fields have an attitude of, "Oh yeah. I've seen this before. I know what to do." And they do it!

I want you to rehearse both mentally and physically. By physically, I mean I want you to rehearse your speech. Rehearse it over and over and over until you almost have it committed to memory.Yes, I know you can't possibly memorize a 15-minute speech. But, if you rehearse it multiple times you will reach the point where all you need to do is see a key word in a paragraph and you'll remember the entire point you were trying to make. Get comfortable with your speech. Get command of your speech.

Your mental rehearsal involves visualization. What's interesting about visualization is that your brain cannot tell the difference whether you are actually doing something or just imagining it. The same emotions and physical responses get triggered. There was a study done on world class sprinters that proves this point. When these sprinters were positioned in their starting blocks and heard the words, "On your mark, set, go!" as they waited to hear the starting gun, certain muscles responded and grew tense. When these same runners were told to imagine the same scenario without really doing it, their muscle response was the same.

So how can you use this phenomenon? If you cannot rehearse at the actual venue, you can rehearse in your mind and your brain will react the same as if you had really been there. Visualize everything you will do on the day of your presentation. See yourself walking into the ballroom or conference room. Imagine yourself enjoying breakfast or lunch at a table of your peers. Hear yourself being introduced and watch yourself make your way from your table to the podium.

Now see yourself confidently delivering the speech you rehearsed over and over and over. And finally, hear the applause as you exit the stage and make your way back to your table.

Visualization is powerful. Do this mental exercise over and over and over until you feel comfortable with your every move. Do this and on the day of the actual presentation you'll be saying to yourself, "Been there, done that!"

Preparation is power! Preparation is your safety net. When you are prepared, you are confident. When you are prepared, you have the attitude that no one knows the information better than you do.

U.S. presidents from John F. Kennedy to the present day not only rehearse their speeches, they also have teleprompter to insure success.

Chapter 30:

Do You Know The Way To San Jose?

"Do you know the way to San Jose..."
Dusty Springfield's 60's hit

I now want you to imagine you're in the room. Visualize the room as clearly as you can – the entryway as you come in, the tables and the stage. I'm going to ask you some questions about the room. There are no wrong answers here. But just by answering the questions you're going to be even further ahead and you're going to be so much more comfortable and confident about your presentation.

First, as you visualize, can you see the stage? Can you see the podium? Got it? OK. Now, try to imagine where you'll be sitting before you give your presentation. Perhaps you're in a conference room where you work and your chair is no more than 20 feet from the podium or lectern where you'll be speaking. Or maybe you're in a ballroom at a table of eight in the middle of the room. Or perhaps you're already seated at the head table up on stage. My point here is I'm not so concerned about where you're sitting. I just want you to be sure that regardless of where you're sitting, you have a route planned out for a graceful and professional-looking entrance. When you are introduced as a speaker and people are clapping, how are you going to get from your table or chair to the podium or lectern? Think it out. Plan it. Leave nothing to chance. Mentally map out your route.

Chapter 31:

Watch Your Step, Your Cell And Don't Be A Heel

If you're in a situation where you'll have to climb a step or two to get up onto the stage and to the podium let me save you some embarrassment. Some stages have steps only on the left side of the stage or only on the right side, but not both. So make sure you know *what* side of the stage the steps are on. There is nothing more embarrassing than being introduced and walking your well-planned route to the stage only to realize there are no steps on the side of the stage you're trying to get up on!

This one's for the ladies. Be sure you know what the *heel* you're doing! I don't need to get into too much detail on this one. Here's a formula for disaster. Two stair steps leading up to the stage, no railing, a nervous woman with speech in hand and high heels!

A collapsed heel, a twisted heel or falling off your heels could result in a fall down the stairs which makes for a really lousy grand entrance!

To save yourself from some on-stage, mid-speech embarrassment, please don't ever (almost never) have your cellphone with you when you're at the podium. Aunt Alice who lives 1000 miles away in Boca Raton doesn't know you're giving a major speech when she calls to tell you Uncle Vinny's gout flared up and she had to take him to the hospital! Let me take this one step further. Even if you leave your cellphone at your table or in your purse, turn it off! If in the middle of your speech you hear a cellphone ring and you realize it's yours, your train of thought and concentration is gone!

Now, in the interest of honesty and full disclosure, I must admit to you that I bring my cellphone to the podium with me every time I do a speech or presentation. But the sound is turned off. I use the cellphone as a clock to make sure my speech is within the allotted time or if I'm emceeing an event it helps me keep things on time and running smoothly.

Chapter 32:

The Microphone Mystery Solved

Here I go again being overly protective of you! I want to tell you about microphones. This may get a little technical and perhaps boring and frankly, you don't really *need* to know this stuff. This is just one more step I'm offering to make sure your big day goes off without a hitch. Perhaps this might convince you to read on –

If you are short, tall, wearing a blouse, a turtleneck, if you don't have pockets, have never done karaoke and don't have three hands, this might be some valuable information!

At most larger venues where speakers make presentations you will have the luxury of choosing from three types of microphones – the lavalier (lav), the wireless handheld and the hardwired. Let me tell you what I like and don't like about each one so that you can determine which one will work best for you and your presentation.

The Lavalier Microphone: The lavalier microphone is simply a microphone that gets clipped onto your lapel and is connected by wire to an audio receiver box which clips on to your back pocket. Imagine having a pack of cigarettes in your back pocket that has a two-foot wire with a clip-on

ne at the end that clips on to your lapel – that's a
microphone or lav.

Pros: The lavalier microphone allows you the most freedom of all the microphone types. Not only can you walk anywhere in the room, but unlike the handheld wireless microphone, the lav leaves both hands free for demonstrations, holding things up for your audience to see or just for effective hand gesturing. In other words, once you have this microphone clipped on and turned on, you don't have to think about it again.

Cons: On the negative side of using a lav, I have found lavs to be the least reliable of all three microphone types. A poor quality lav or a lav that is clipped too low on your lapel – in other words, too far from your voice box especially in the case of a softer-voiced person – can lead to poor sound quality. Trust me, nothing will rattle you more than getting 20 seconds into your speech or presentation and you hear several people in the audience shouting, "Can't hear you!" At this point one of four things will happen – all of which will absolutely ruin your big opening. First, SM (Stage Manager) rushes onto the stage to move the microphone on your lapel so that it's closer to your voicebox. Second, SM reaches into your back pocket, pulls out the receiver box and checks to see if the battery is low. Third, if SM determines there is something wrong with your lavalier microphone, he will switch you to a handheld or a hardwired microphone which *really* throws you off because you hadn't planned on dealing with the nuanaces of those two microphones. Fourth and finally, SM will try to set you up with a new lavalier microphone which is physically impossible! Why impossible? Ideally, you have to put on your lavalier microphone long before your speech. Not only does the receiver box have to be clipped to a back or front pocket, but the wearer has to run the microphone wire up underneath his or her shirt or blouse so that the wire is not visible. Try pullin' that off live on stage! And remember, not a lot of ladies who are at an event where they'll be delivering a speech have pockets!My best advice here is if you want to use a lavalier microphone, get to the venue early, have the SM clip it on your lapel and back pocket and then test it – listen to how it sounds. *This* is the time to work out the bugs and *not* during your speech.

The Wireless Handheld: If you've done karaoke then you have used a wireless handheld microphone. This is the microphone that all the pop stars, entertainers and TV game show hosts use. It's about the size of a bottle of beer, it's got a battery inside so there are no wires and your hand fits comfortably around it, just like a bottle of beer!

Pros: As with the lavalier microphone, the wireless handheld microphone gives you the freedom to move about the room. You've also got one hand free for demonstrations, holding up objects and for gesturing.

Cons: The most obvious negative is the fact that you have just one hand free and that can limit what you're able to do in your presentation. If you need two hands to hold up or demonstrate a larger item you could run into a problem. The other problem is one you can prove to yourself at home. Hold a beer bottle in one hand and in the other hand hold a five-page speech. Alright, you've read to the bottom of page one and it's time to turn to page two. How are you going to do it? You can't! Not gracefully, anyway. When using a wireless handheld microphone it's best that you lay your speech on the podium so that when it comes time to turn the page you only need one hand to do it. Also, always keep the mic close to your mouth. If you turn your head to the left or to the right and don't keep the mic right at your mouth, your audience will miss some words. Keep the mic at your mouth no matter where your head turns.

See, I'm takin' care of ya! Remember, all these pitfalls I'm warning you against – I've done 'em all!

One more thing about a wireless handheld microphone. If during the course of your speech you happen to give special recognition to someone that will elicit applause, *you* can't clap. Go ahead, hold a beer bottle and try it!

The Hardwired Podium Microphone: This is the microphone that is inserted into that gooseneck arm attached to the podium. It is the microphone that stares you in the face as you approach the podium.

Pros: Unlike the lavalier and handheld wireless microphones that rely on batteries, hardwired microphones don't fail. They're plugged into the room's power source so unless there's a power outage you'll have nothing to worry about. Both hands are free for demonstrations, turning pages, clapping and gesturing. You also may experience a sense of security standing behind a solid podium –all of your 'stuff' is right there in front of you and you've also got something to hang onto both physically and psychologically.

Cons: The biggest negative about the hardwired podium microphone is that you're stuck at the podium and cannot move about the room. Second, you must make sure that the podium microphone is directly in line with your mouth and you must stay close to it as you speak. If you tilt your head down to read your speech or if you look left or right you will hear those nightmarish words, "Can't hear you!"

Chapter 33:

Soundcheck Like A Rockstar!

Have you ever been to a rock concert? I have. More than I can remember, dating back to the late 60's and early 70's – Kiss, Alice Cooper, Jethro Tull, Yes, Humble Pie, Savoy Brown, Scorpions, Cheap Trick, Johnny Winter, Mountain and Foghat to name a few. I admit it, I even saw The Monkees!

While each concert had its own unique vibe or flavor depending upon the artist, they all had one thing in common – top quality sound. Long before the concert-goers arrived, the roadies spent the better part of the day doing a sound check to make sure the microphones, amplifiers, instruments and foldback speakers were properly set. In fact, once the roadies have completed their work, the band itself will often test everything. It's better to uncover problems in an empty arena rather than when the lights come up and the real show starts.

No band on earth would simply walk out on stage before 10,000 screaming fans without first having done a complete sound check. To skip the sound check would be suicide.

You may not be a rock star, but on the day of your presentation you are definitely the star. Just as is the case with your musical counterparts, skipping a sound check is inviting disaster.

Chapter 34:

Hey, I Sound Pretty Good!

Whichever microphone you choose to use, ask SM to take you through a sound check. Rock bands, country bands and Broadway performers all insist on sound checks. As I noted earlier, these professionals would never step out on stage in front of 10,000 people before making sure the sound was perfect! Your sound check will take no more than a minute. SM will turn your microphone on and your job is to speak into it just as you would during your actual presentation. This simple exercise will pay off tenfold because it will give you a feel for how you're going to sound, what your voice sounds like as it carries through the room and what it actually feels like to use the microphone you've chosen.

Do you see what we're doing here? I'm having you live the experience of your speech before you actually do it. That way, when it's time for the real presentation, your brain says, "Oh, yeah. I've been here before. I know what's going to happen. I know what to do."

Chapter 35:

Turn Me On

On the day of your presentation find your friend SM and ask him to turn your microphone on *for you*. You won't have to worry about this if you are using the hardwired microphone affixed to the podium. It's the lavalier and the wireless handheld microphones that have all kinds of hidden booby traps when it comes to trying to turn them on. Remember the cigarette-pack sized receiver box for the lav microphone, the one that clips to your back pocket? It's got a tiny on-off switch. Trust me, unless you've got hands and fingers the size of a five-year-old, turning the switch to the 'on' position is nearly impossible. Not to mention you'd have to unclip the box from your back pocket in order to turn the switch on and then re-clip the box as you make your way to the stage. Not gonna happen! Make sure your microphone is on well before your speech. I've seen too many SM's tell a speaker, "All ya gotta do is hit this 'on' switch." Never works. And when it inevitably doesn't work, SM has to come running up on stage, pull the box out of your back pocket, turn it on and then jam it down into your back pocket again. So much for your grand entrance!

It's the same situation with handheld microphones. Most handhelds have a simple on and off switch which isn't too hard to figure out. However, in this day of high technology, some handhelds have a button on the bottom of the microphone which you must press and hold for two seconds before the microphone is activated. This seemingly simple press-and-hold technique works very well when SM does it. But when you do it – nothing. That's the point where SM rushes the stage, presses the button, the microphone comes to life and you look like an idiot. Again, so much for your grand entrance! It's like competing in a 100-yard dash and when the starting gun goes off you stumble out of the starting blocks. Bottom line – make sure any microphone you are using is turned on ahead of time. You've got your hands full enough with your speech. Leave the audio to the experts.

Chapter 36:

A Final Soundoff About Sound

I know it seems like I've gone into way too much detail about the intricacies of the different microphones. And while I'm sorry if I may have bored you I did it for your own good. Sound is everything! Without sound there is no presentation. You can have the most top-quality, state-of-the-art microphones at your disposal but if you don't know how to use them properly you might as well use string and two Dixie cups! Finally, I want you to understand that when there's an audio problem because somebody didn't check things ahead of time, it should make you mad as heck! Because when the audience shouts, "Can't hear you!" – do you know what they're really saying? They're saying, "It was all for nothing. All your worry, all the time you spent writing the speech, all the time you spent rehearsing it, it was all for nothing because no one is hearing it except you!"

Chapter 37:

Let There Be Light

A very important thing I want you to check with SM on is lighting. When your convention dinner is underway the room is flooded with light making you believe you'll have no problem reading your speech when you get on stage. You've been to convention dinners and speeches before. What happens when dinner wraps up and it's time for the program on stage to begin? The house lights go down, right? So, I want you to leave nothing to chance. Find out from SM if there is a light shining down on the podium from above, and I don't mean some dim light 20 feet above your head – that's not going to help you. If the ceiling light is too high and doesn't provide the light you need there is one thing you can do to make sure lighting will not be a problem. Insist on a light *on* the podium – a light that works!

I learned this lesson the hard way early in my career. As I was getting ready to deliver my speech the house lights dimmed to near darkness. I noticed the light on the podium wasn't plugged into an outlet so I quickly found SM and asked him to plug it in. I approached the podium and turned the light switch on. Nothing. At which point I realized there was no bulb! I've even gone so far as to leave the stage. I looked for the brightest light in the room and I went over and stood under it! I don't want that happen to you. Check everything ahead of time and leave nothing to chance.

Bottom line – make sure there is a light on the podium and make sure someone has turned it on for you ahead of time.

Chapter 38:

"You Can't Have 'Dem Lights!"

Talk about not checking lighting! This is a true story of something that happened early in my television career that taught me the value of paying attention to detail and preparing for anything.

It was February 26, 1976. I was a 23-year old graduate student at Marshall University in Huntington, West Virginia. I was asked to host a live television broadcast that would feature former Israeli Defense Minister Moshe Dayan. At the time, Dayan was a lightning rod when it came to Middle East tensions. It was he who masterminded Israel's victory in the 1967 Six Day War over Egypt, Jordan and Syria. Dayan's trademark was a patch over one eye that he lost in battle.

Dayan's appearance was of such import at the time that we were informed that not only would West Virginia Governor Jay Rockefeller be watching but also White House televisions would be tuned in. This, by the way, was my first live television appearance ever!

The room was filled with 1000 people. Security was everywhere. On stage was a podium from which Dayan would speak. Bright lights flooded the stage for this momentous event.

Ten minutes before air time I could hear loud voices coming from the front of the stage. There was an argument of some sort. I could hear a man speaking in broken English loudly exclaiming, "You can't have 'dem lights! You can't have 'dem lights!" It was an Israeli security agent, one of Dayan's bodyguards and it was obvious by the way his trenchcoat bulged he was heavily armed. His tirade was aimed at our stage manager/producer Dave. The security agent persisted, "You can't have 'dem lights!"

I approached the two men to find out what the problem was. The security agent calmed down a bit and explained that since Dayan could only see out of one eye, the bright, blinding stage lighting would make it difficult for Dayan to see someone in the crowd who might jump up with a gun in an assassination attempt. Dayan wouldn't have time to react, duck and save himself.

After some delicate negotiations and a resetting of a few lights, the agent was satisfied that the man who's life he was to protect would be safe.

With microphone in hand I took my position at the door to the stage and announced the impending entrance of Moshe Dayan. The door opened and I found myself face-to-face with the patch. Mr. Dayan smiled at me, I smiled back and gestured him to the podium.

International incident avoided. Lesson in lighting learned.

Chapter 39:

Take A Stand, Then Take A Bow

You are now armed with everything you need to take the next step in your public speaking journey. You confronted the emotional, mental and physical components of dealing with the fear of public speaking and you're still standing. You made it!Take a bow.

As we talked about earlier in this book you are only going to need about twenty percent of what you've learned here to make your next and subsequent speeches successful.

But just having the information isn't enough. Now you've got to do something with it.

You have a lethal weapon in your arsenal, so use it. I think you'd agree it would be insanity for a man with an AK-47 to stand passively and do nothing while several people try to drown him with squirt guns!

The information you now have is your AK-47. The people you were afraid to speak in front of are holding squirt guns. Pull the imaginary trigger! It's time to take a stand.

You now know that your fear about public speaking was an inside job. The fear came from within you. Your fears were the result of wrong perceptions about yourself and your audience. There is no 'out there'. No one is out there criticizing you and no one out there wants you to fail. It's just the opposite. The 'out there' is in awe of you. The 'out there' wishes they had the nerve and know-how to do what you can do. The 'out there' is envious of you.

I truly hope you have enjoyed our time together and that you will refer to parts of this book anytime you need a little motivation or support. You are a new person. I leave you with a quote reported to have been spoken by Japanese Admiral Yamamoto, the man who planned the attack on Pearl Harbor on December 7, 1941. As he looked out over Pearl Harbor and saw the devastation his forces had delivered, he said:

"I fear we have awakened a sleeping giant and filled him with a terrible resolve."

Resolve to Leave 'Em Speechless!

Other Books By Tom Zalaski

The View From The Blanket – Weekapaug

If you own a cottage or have ever rented one at the ocean, the lake, a river or a resort get ready to relive the experience each time you open *The View From The Blanket*. Year 'round therapy to get you through your worst winter day at the office.

We Need To Do A Benefit Fundraiser – But How?

A loved one or friend is in need of financial help due to an illness, tragedy or unforeseen circumstance and you have taken it upon yourself to lead the way to get that person on their feet physically and financially. This is the step-by-step how-to book to coordinate that all-important benefit fundraiser.

How To Manipulate The Media For Fun And Profit

How to deal with the media in good times and bad. Media strategy for when your company has a strike, a stockholder revolt, a scandal, a product recall and even an accidental death. Also, how to get the media to cover your 'good stuff' like the check presentation, a groundbreaking, new product unveil and employee community involvement. Tips from Tom Zalaski from his 40 years of anchoring television newscasts!

Available at:
Amazon.com
Amazon kindle
Barnes and Noble
www.tomzalaski.com

17601176R00070

Printed in Great Britain
by Amazon